Cookies!

Cookies!

Irresistible recipes for cookies,
bars, squares and slices

Pippa Cuthbert & Lindsay Cameron Wilson

Good Books

Intercourse, PA 17534
800/762-7171
www.GoodBooks.com

Dedication
To the Charlies, the cookie lovers of the future!

First published in North America by Good Books
Intercourse, PA 17534
800/762/7171
www.GoodBooks.com

COOKIES!
Good Books, Intercourse, PA 17534

International Standard Book Number: 978-1-56148-556-7;
1-56148-556-X (paperback)
International Standard Book Number: 978-1-56148-557-4;
1-56148-557-8 (comb-bound)

Library of Congress Catalog Card Number: 2006024678

Library of Congress Cataloging-in-Publication Data

Cuthbert, Pippa.
   Cookies! : irresistible recipes for cookies, bars, squares
   and slices / Pippa Cuthbert & Lindsay Cameron Wilson.
        p. cm.
Includes bibliographical references and index.
   ISBN-13: 978-1-56148-556-7 (pbk.)
   ISBN-13: 978-1-56148-557-4 (comb)
1. Cookies. I. Wilson, Lindsay Cameron. II. Title.
   TX772.C88 2007
   641.8'654--dc22
                                    2006024678

Editor: Ruth Hamilton and Anna Bennett
Design: Paul Wright
Photography: Stuart West
Food styling: Pippa Cuthbert
Production: Hazel Kirkman
Editorial Direction: Rosemary Wilkinson

Reproduction by Pica Digital PTE Ltd, Singapore
Printed and bound in China by C&C Offset

Acknowledgments
Many thanks to Julia Leonard at Divertimenti
(www.divertimenti.co.uk) and Lindy Wiffen at Ceramica Blue
(www.ceramicablue.co.uk) for their gorgeous props.
Thanks also to all our family and friends who shared countless
recipes and coveted cookie secrets with us.
Thanks to Stuart West, our tireless photographer, for his
discerning palate and fabulous photography.
And many thanks to Rosie and Eric at Books for Cooks
(www.booksforcooks.com) for their continued support.

Both metric and imperial measures are given for the recipes –
follow either set of measures, but not a mixture of both as they
are not interchangeable.

NOTE
The author and publishers have made every effort to ensure that
all instructions given in this book are safe and accurate, but they
cannot accept liability for any resulting injury or loss or damage to
either property or person, whether direct or consequential and
howsoever arising.

Contents

Introduction

It's a cold and wintry day outside, but I have a cup of tea and chocolate cookies to keep me warm. These cookies, Mary's cookies, aren't your average chocolate cookies. They are made in a saucepan on the stove, with just a handful of simple ingredients. Chocolate is melted with butter, milk and vanilla extract. Oats and coconut are added and everything is stirred together until it forms a smooth mass. The mixture is spooned onto parchment-lined baking sheets, and the cookies are chilled until firm. Strangely enough, the poor things don't even have a name. Some call them "no-bake chocolate cookies." Boring. I've heard them called "chocolate macaroons," but really, everyone knows macaroons are baked. I recently heard them called "frogs," which doesn't make any sense whatsoever, but it's the most interesting name I've heard, so that's what they will be. I try to let my "frogs" firm in the fridge, but I can't wait that long. The cookies are warm and perfect for eating. As I scoop a frog from the baking

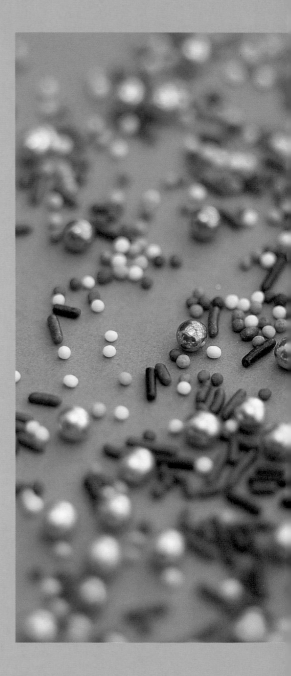

parchment, I look over my shoulder. A smear of chocolate is left where the cookie should be, and there's no way I can cover my tracks. My mother will know that I helped myself to a cookie before they were ready. But hey, am I not the mother now, and can't I do whatever I want? I haven't tasted these divine little memories for what seems like forever, and I think I deserve this little indulgence.

I found the recipe for this cookie on a faded page in my mother's recipe collection. When she heard that Pippa and I were about to embark on a cookie book, she promptly brought it over. It's a hard-covered black notebook that is just as much a journal as it is a recipe collection. The corners are curled and the spine has long since disappeared. The recipes inside chronicle decades of family meals, the evolution of her cooking, and the people with whom she shared recipes. I open the book and a frail, faded page falls to the floor. The book isn't that old, but it has had a rough life: it has survived a flood, a

house fire, many moves and countless sticky fingers. The first page, however, is surprisingly clear. It is a recipe for Mary's chocolate cookies, given to her in 1974 by our neighbor Mary McNamara. We moved away from Mary's neighborhood in 1976, and Mary passed away several years ago. But her memory enters my mother's kitchen every time one of Mary's recipes is being made. Today, her memory is here in my kitchen.

That is the beauty of baking cookies. The aroma wafts through the kitchen, creating a familiar warmth that transports us to another time, another place. This may sound overly quaint and archaic in the fast-food, post-feminist world in which we live. But the immediate satisfaction of cookie making slides into modern life perfectly. A cookie can be conceived, whipped up, baked and eaten within 30 minutes. A frilly apron isn't even required. Before we know it we are comforted, and in turn, we can comfort others.

Cookie comfort comes in many forms. Some people require a daily fix of chocolate. Others simply want a crisp ginger cookie to dunk into a cup of tea. Then there are those who reserve cookie comfort for specific times of the year – shortbread at Christmas, chocolate cookies on Valentine's Day, lemon wafers at Easter. These are times for slightly fancier cookies and indulgent ingredients. The more important the celebration, the more splendid the cookie, you see. These kinds of cookies not only trigger memories, they reinforce the celebration itself.

English-turned-Canadian writer Margaret Visser writes about the connection between food and custom in her book *The Rituals of Dinner*: "Feasts, by means of structure and ritual, deliberately use the powerful connotations of food to recall origins and earlier times. They also attempt to be events in themselves unforgettable, in order to furnish recollections for the future. The food served at festivals is, therefore, not only richer and more splendid than what we usually eat, but also traditional, inherited from the past and intended to be experienced as ancient custom; the recipes and the lore associated with it are to be handed on by us for use again in ritual celebrations."

I don't think Visser would mind if I replace *cookies* for feasts. Cookies recall origins of earlier times; they attempt to be events in themselves and they furnish recollections for the future. That is quite a lot for a humble little cookie.

The name cookie derives from the Dutch *koekje*, a diminutive of the word *koek*, meaning cake. *Koek* eventually became the English *cookie*. Funnily enough, the name *cookie* is almost exclusively used by North Americans, while the English and French call them *biscuits*. *Biscuit* comes from the French words *bis*, meaning twice, and *cuit*, meaning cooked, which is how biscuits were originally made. This explains the crisp quality of a biscuit. They snap, they crunch and they are delicious dunked in tea. A cookie, on the other hand, is traditionally a free-form drop of dough that is baked just once. The name has evolved to include every kind of "cookie," from drop to rolled, pressed to refrigerated. Bars, squares and slices also come under the category of cookie.

Whichever way you slice it, the tiny cookie carries a great deal of weight. Cookies can represent a country, a celebration, a memory or an event. Their ingredients can be varied according to mood, their flavors shifted according to trends, tastes or availability. They are deceptively easy while simultaneously impressive. That's why Pippa and I love them. They fulfill our varied tastes. They satisfy our cravings. They allow us to celebrate recipes from the past.

Making cookies

There are five main methods for making cookies. The chosen method basically comes down to the type of cookie you are trying to make and is determined by the way in which the butter is incorporated into the mixture. Below we explain the different techniques, and at least one of the methods will apply to each and every recipe that follows.

THE CREAMING METHOD

The creaming method is probably the most common cookie-making method. It involves beating the butter and sugar together until pale, creamy and fluffy in texture. Always use softened butter that has ideally been out of the fridge for at least 30 minutes. The eggs are always added to the creamed mixture before the dry ingredients. Always keep your eggs at room temperature to avoid them curdling with the butter and sugar. If any curdling does occur, add a couple of tablespoons of flour to the mixture before adding the remaining egg or liquid. For ease and speed we often refer to using the beaters of an electric mixer for this method, but a wooden spoon and a bit of arm power will do the job just as well.

Examples of cookies that use the creaming method are Chocolate chip cookies and Chocolate Afghans.

THE RUBBING METHOD

For this method the butter should be cool and firm but not straight from the fridge. Try removing the butter from the fridge about 5 minutes before you need it and cut it into small cubes. In this method the butter is added to the flour and rubbed using your fingertips until it resembles the texture of fine breadcrumbs. The sugar is then added and combined before the addition of any other liquid ingredients. The mixture will come together to form a firm dough and will hold together in a ball. The dough can then be rolled out and cut into cookie shapes. Sometimes the dough will need to be chilled before it is rolled, but the recipe will always specify when this is necessary. If it is a particularly warm day, you may wish to do this anyway to ease the process.

This method also works successfully using a food processor. Put the flour and other dry ingredients in the food processor and pulse several times to combine the ingredients. Sprinkle in the cubed butter and pulse several more times (about 10 seconds) until the mixture resembles the texture of fine breadcrumbs. Remove the mixture at this stage and add the liquid ingredients, using a wooden spoon to combine. You do not want to over-mix the mixture by adding the liquid ingredients to the food processor. Mix into a ball and continue as instructed in the recipe.

Examples of cookies that use this method are Sugar butter cookies.

THE MELTING METHOD
This method begins with the butter and sugar (or other sweeteners such as honey or corn syrup) being melted in a saucepan over gentle heat. The dry ingredients are then added to the liquid mixture to form a soft dough. The dough is then shaped and baked, often resulting in a crisp end product.

Examples of cookies using this method are Gingernuts and Flapjacks.

THE WHISKING METHOD
This method begins with the eggs and, more often than not, sugar being whisked together. The dry ingredients are then gently folded into the egg mixture, trying to keep it as light and aerated as possible. The result is usually a delicate and crisp, wafer-like biscuit.

Examples of cookies using this method are *Tuiles*, Fortune cookies and *Langues de chat*.

THE ALL-IN-ONE METHOD
This straightforward method requires the fat to be soft enough to blend easily. All the ingredients are placed in one bowl or food processor and beaten until just combined. It is important not to over-beat the mixture. Chunky ingredients, such as chocolate chips or nuts, should be stirred in at the end.

Ingredients

BUTTER

Butter is the best fat for cookie making, not only for its consistency and texture but also, ultimately, for its flavor. Unsalted and salted butter are both called for in our recipes, but unsalted is often the preferred choice for cookie making (when not specified, always choose unsalted butter for baking). It is the temperature of butter that is important when making cookies. For the creaming method, it should be at room temperature or soft enough to mix easily with the sugar. Remove the butter from the fridge at least 30 minutes before baking for this method. For the rubbed method, the butter should be cold and firm but not straight from the fridge. Ideally remove it from the fridge about 5 minutes before you need it. Other fat alternatives to butter are margarine, oil and lard. The most notable difference when using these fats will be the flavor.

SUGAR OR OTHER SWEETENERS

Extra-fine sugar

The smaller crystals or finer grains of extra-fine sugar allow it to incorporate more air than other sugars, which makes it perfect for creating a light, fluffy mixture such as you would obtain using the creaming method. The finer grains also dissolve faster, making it ideal in the melting method.

Granulated sugar

Granulated sugar has larger granules and is often used in rubbed cookie mixtures or to make a crunchy sugar topping.

Vanilla sugar

Commercial vanilla sugar is made by adding vanilla extract or vanilla seeds to extra-fine sugar. It is simpler and less expensive to make your own: just add a vanilla pod to an airtight jar filled with extra-fine sugar and allow the flavor and aroma to infuse for at least a week.

Brown sugar

When a richer caramel or molasses flavor is desired, we have used a variety of brown sugars: soft brown sugar (light or dark), demerara (larger crystals), molasses sugar or muscovado (light or dark) sugars. Brown sugars are white sugar with molasses added.

Confectioners sugar
Confectioners sugar is the powdery, brilliant-white sugar that dissolves instantly when mixed with liquid. It is ideal for dusting over cookies once cooked or in icings and glazes. Some cookies use confectioners sugar in the dough, which results in a more crumbly, textured result.

Corn syrup
Corn syrup has a honey-like texture and is a byproduct of the sugar-refining process. It adds a distinctive flavor and color to your baking.

Maple syrup
Look for maple syrup that has a maple leaf symbol on the label: this guarantees the product's authenticity and its origin. Avoid any "maple-flavored" products if you can. Maple syrup is the boiled-down sap of certain kinds of maple trees native to the United States and Canada. It gives a sweetness and yet another distinctive flavor.

Honey
The flavor and aroma of honey depends entirely on the flowers from which the nectar has been obtained. Single-flower honeys are generally the best, although some honeys from mixed flowers can also be good – it is all a question of personal taste. The general rule is the darker the honey the stronger the flavor, so choose a honey based on how dominant you want the flavor to be.

FLOUR
There are two main types of wheat grown today: hard and soft, each with a characteristic kernel composition and each with its own particular culinary use. The wheat kernel will vary in "hardness" – the measure of protein content, which in turn determines the flour's gluten content. Hard flour contains large protein chunks and relatively little starch. As a result, this flour forms a strong gluten when mixed with water and it is thus commonly used in bread making. Soft flours, on the other hand, contain less protein and a higher starch content and consequently develop

a weaker gluten. Soft flours are more commonly used for baking and cakes where the texture is meant to be more tender and crumbly.

The following is a simple guide to the different flours available and their uses:

All-purpose flour

This is the flour used in almost all of our cookie recipes. Whenever possible choose a grade 00 (the Italian *doppio zero*, double zero) flour, the finest all-purpose flour available, and the one which consequently contains the least gluten. This flour does not require sifting, although sifting is a good habit to get into as it is necessary for all other flours. A harder, or grade 1, flour is also suitable for baking, but the gluten level is higher and will produce a less

crumbly end product. Do not use bread flour for making cookies.

Self-rising flour

This flour contains raising agents that make cookies and cakes spread and rise, giving them a lighter texture. If you do not have self-rising flour, add 1 teaspoon of baking powder to 5½oz (150g) all-purpose flour and combine well. Self-rising flour should not be kept for longer than three months as the raising agents will deteriorate.

Cornmeal (polenta)

A coarse grain produced from the hardest kind of wheat grown today. It is generally too hard for cookie and cake making on its own but can be added to doughs for texture and crunch.

Cornstarch

Cornstarch is a fine white powder that is often added to cookie mixtures to give a smooth and slightly crumbly texture.

Rice flour/potato flour

These are good substitutes for anyone who has a gluten or wheat intolerance and will often result in a crumblier texture.

RAISING AGENTS

Cookies require raising agents that are fast acting. Compare this to the bread-making process where the raising agent yeast produces CO_2 at a relatively slow rate. In bread making the dough is manipulated enough to allow the gluten to develop. The gluten is in a continuous phase and will continue to expand with the production of CO_2. In cookie making the production of CO_2 is also required to raise the product. The raising is a result of a chemical reaction between acidic and alkaline compounds, and this is where baking powder and baking soda come into action.

Baking soda

Baking soda is an alkaline component and is almost totally made of sodium bicarbonate ($NaHCO_3$, or bicarbonate of soda). It is used when the dough or batter is already acidic enough to react with the baking soda to form CO_2. It requires another acidic ingredient, such as buttermilk or yogurt, to be present for the reaction to occur. If the dough or batter is not acidic enough, then baking powder will be called for.

Baking powder

Baking powder contains baking soda and an acid in the form of salt crystals that dissolve in water. Baking powder compensates for the lack of acid in the dough or batter and itself will form a reaction to produce CO_2. A home version of baking powder can be made by mixing ¼ teaspoon baking soda with ½ teaspoon cream of tartar; this is roughly equivalent to 1 teaspoon baking powder.

EGGS

For simplicity's sake we have used large eggs, average weight 2¼–2½oz (65–70g), throughout the book. If you find you have an excess of egg whites in your fridge, then put them in a bag and freeze them, clearly marking the date and number of whites. Use them within four months. Allow the white to defrost overnight in the fridge or under hot running water and use immediately once defrosted. Frozen eggs should only be used for recipes in which the white is thoroughly cooked.

Separating eggs

Many of our recipes require only an egg yolk or a white. It is easy to separate an egg: tap the middle of the egg sharply against the rim of

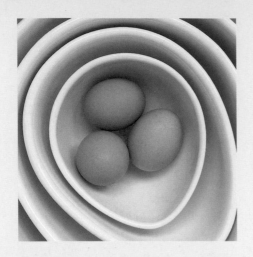

a glass bowl or against the center of another egg. Holding the egg over the bowl, gently pull the shell apart with the tips of your thumbs. Carefully let the white drain into the bowl while you tip the yolk from one half shell to the other.

CHOCOLATE

Chocolate is obtained from the cocoa bean, which has been roasted, cracked then husked to expose the nibs. The nibs are then ground with water to produce the cocoa liquor or mass. This cocoa mass can then be further reduced to produce cocoa butter and cocoa powder. It is the percentage of cocoa mass or cocoa solids in chocolate that gives it its taste.

Bittersweet and unsweetened baking chocolate

Unsweetened baking chocolate can generally be made up of up

to 95% cocoa solids with no added sugar. This chocolate is extremely bitter, glossy, smooth and almost red in color. It melts easily and snaps cleanly.

Bittersweet chocolate has the addition of sugar and a lower cocoa solids percentage, usually about 50%–70% cocoa solids.

We recommend the use of Lindt chocolate (available worldwide) and also Green & Blacks, which is becoming more universally available.

Milk chocolate

Milk chocolate has milk solids and sugar added to it, giving it a lower percentage of cocoa solids – usually about 10%–30%. It is sweeter and creamier in texture, with a less intense chocolate taste. We find that children often prefer this less bitter alternative, particularly in ice cream.

White chocolate

Technically white chocolate is not chocolate at all. White chocolate only contains cocoa butter, milk solids and sugar, no cocoa solids. Vanilla flavoring is often added so look for quality clues on the label, such as "natural" or "pure." White chocolate is not as

readily interchangeable as other chocolate. It must be treated more delicately as it has a tendency to seize.

Chocolate chips/chunks

These tiny morsels of chocolate are perfect for cookie making. They melt easily and are generally more stable than the bar versions of the same chocolate. Be sure to buy chocolate chips made from real chocolate if you can. Alternatively, buy chocolate bars and cut them into chunks.

Cocoa powder

Cocoa is a byproduct of chocolate. It is the other product, along with cocoa butter, that is produced when the cocoa solids or cocoa liquor are pressed during the manufacture of chocolate. Cocoa is its dried, powdered form and has no added sugar. It has a final fat content of between 10%–35%.

FRUIT

Dried fruit is more intense in flavor than fresh fruit. It does not affect the moisture content of the dough so it is usually possible to substitute one dried fruit for another. Apricots, apples, pears and raisins are widely available, although these days it is often possible to find a good selection of tropical fruits and summer berries as well.

Candied and crystalized fruit

Although you can make this yourself, it is a long process and can sometimes work out to be more expensive than buying it ready-made. The process of crystalizing means that the fruits retain their bright colors and can be used for decorative purposes. It is better to buy whole pieces of candied or crystalized fruit and chop them yourself to prevent drying out.

Fresh

Fresh fruit varies considerably in moisture content so it is not as easy to substitute one for another. Fruits such as citrus fruits are often used for their juice and rind rather than their flesh.

NUTS

Nuts can be stirred into cookie doughs before cooking, sprinkled over uncooked doughs or used as decoration on icings or glazes. Always buy whole fresh nuts and chop them as required. They turn rancid relatively quickly, so store well in an airtight container and use as quickly as possible.

SEEDS

Seeds are particularly popular in muesli bars and flapjacks, where a wholesome, high-energy product is desired.

SPICES AND HERBS

Spices and herbs are often added to cookies and are an easy way to add flavor. Sweet cookies usually use warm spices such as cinnamon, nutmeg or ginger in their dried, ground forms. Vanilla is probably the spice that is most frequently added to cookies and imparts a fragrant, delicate flavor. Herbs are usually added to savory cookies or biscuits, although herbs such as rosemary and mint will be found in some sweet cookie recipes.

Vanilla pod

The pod is from a climbing orchid plant native to Central America. Good-quality pods should be deep brown in color and soft, not hard. Vanilla pods have a warm and perfumed fragrant aroma and taste.

Vanilla extract

When time and money are limited, your next best alternative to a vanilla pod is vanilla extract – the "pure" and "natural" distilled extract from the pod. The word "extract" ensures that the product is derived from the vanilla pod. Avoid any imitation or synthetic vanilla "essences." It is the flavor of essences that is used in most cheap ice creams and it leaves a lingering, artificial flavor. Vanilla essence is often made from just one component of vanilla extract – vanillin. It is vanillin in combination with other substances such as gums, resins and oils that make the extract.

If in doubt, always check the bottle for words such as "extract," "pure," and "natural," and avoid any product labelled "essence," "synthetic," or "imitation."

FLAVORED WATERS

Rosewater is made from the distillation of rose petals and is commonly used in the Middle East and India to flavor both sweet and savory dishes. This should be available at your local supermarket and can usually be found in the baking section.

Orange flower water (also known as orange blossom water) is made from the distillation of orange blossoms. Like rosewater, this should be available from the baking section of your local supermarket.

Equipment

BOWLS

Invest in a set of bowls in varying sizes: large ones for mixing doughs and smaller ones for measuring individual ingredients. Ensure that they are heatproof so that they can be used over a double boiler or for melting butter and chocolate in the microwave. We like to use glass or Pyrex bowls, which are extremely multi-functional.

MEASURING CUPS/SPOONS

Exact measurements are essential in baking so we encourage investing in an accurate, commercially produced set of each before attempting our recipes. Always level off the top of your spoons using the back of a knife or a palette knife. When measuring brown sugar, it should be lightly packed into the spoon and then leveled off. If you are measuring hot liquids, use a glass or Pyrex cup that will neither melt nor conduct heat. When measuring liquids, always bring yourself down to eye level with the top of the liquid level to check the accuracy of your measure.

Measurements:
1 tsp = 5 ml (liquid) =
  1 level teaspoon
1 Tbsp = 15ml (liquid) =
  3 level teaspoons

SCALES

It is necessary to own a set of scales with both imperial and metric measures. The most technically advanced and efficient are electronic scales, usually battery-operated, that enable you to switch from metric to imperial at the press of a button. This can be a useful function, but never jump between metric and imperial measurements in one recipe – it won't work – stick strictly to one or the other system. The main advantage of electric scales is that they can be re-set to zero after each ingredient is added. Balance scales require two sets of weights (one for metric and one for imperial). They can be attractive but will take up a lot more space in your kitchen. Scales vary in their maximum weighing capacity, so make sure you invest in a set that suits your particular needs.

SIFTERS

It is useful to have a large and a small sifter for cookie making. Make sure that they are strong and have a fine mesh. Use the large sifter for sifting dry ingredients such as flour and the small sifter for dusting icing sugar or cocoa powder over cookies.

WHISKS

Wire balloon whisks in a large and small size will be all you need. They are useful for whisking egg whites and whipping cream and can also be useful to help remove lumps from confectioners sugar. There is also the old-fashioned hand-held rotary whisk, which will help speed things up without having to resort to the electric version.

ELECTRIC MIXERS

We mention these in many of our recipes, but don't forget that whisking can often be done using hand-held balloon whisks or hand-held rotary whisks or even a wooden spoon. Electric mixers are useful for whisking egg whites and creaming butter and sugar, but remember always to fold the dry ingredients in by hand. Cookie doughs can easily be over-mixed, which will spoil the final texture. Electric whisks are also useful in that they can be used in a saucepan over heat. Choose one with three different speeds and beaters that can be easily removed and washed.

PALETTE KNIVES/SPATULAS (METAL AND RUBBER)

Palette knives are very useful tools that have many uses. They are a simple and easy way to level off teaspoon measures. Also, use them to transfer cut cookie shapes from the worktop or cutting board to the baking sheet and again to a wire cooling rack. Choose a couple of different sizes and knives that are flexible enough to bend under pressure. Rubber spatulas should also be flexible to enable them to remove every last bit of cookie dough from the mixing bowl. Metal and rubber spatulas are also useful for folding dry ingredients into a creamed or whisked mixture.

BAKING PARCHMENT

Baking parchment is a siliconized baking paper that enables you to bake cookies and cakes without having to grease the tray or sheet. Alternatively, you can purchase re-usable baking sheets, which are also siliconized and just need to be wiped clean between each use. If you have no baking parchment, the best alternative is to grease your baking sheet lightly with butter or oil or choose a non-stick baking sheet.

WIRE RACKS

Wire racks are essential for cooling cookies and preventing them from going soft or continuing to cook and becoming too crisp. This is because they allow the air to circulate. Once cooked, some cookies should be left for a couple of minutes to firm up before being transferred to the rack. Once completely cool, cookies should immediately be transferred to an airtight container for storage.

ROLLING PINS

Rolling pins come in all shapes and sizes. Some have handles and others don't. Most rolling pins are either wooden or marble, and child-sized rolling pins are available too. Choose whatever is most comfortable for you.

TIMERS

It's important to time your cookies while baking, as all recipes are tested and cooking times are given for a reason. One or two minutes too long may result in over-baked or burnt cookies. Most modern ovens are fitted with a timer, but if you are without one, it is well worth investing in one. The simple dial timers, which usually time up to 60 minutes, are both cheap and perfectly adequate for cookie making. Modern, digital timers are even more accurate but consequently more expensive as well.

PIPING BAGS

It is worthwhile having a selection of different-sized piping bags with a selection of tips. Large piping bags are useful for piping uncooked cookie dough onto trays. Smaller piping bags come in handy when you want to add decorative finishing touches with icing or buttercream. Piping bags these days are generally made of nylon. Choose one that is double-stitched down the seams. Disposable piping bags can also be purchased or, alternatively, use a small plastic bag with the corner snipped off if none of the above are available.

COOKIE CUTTERS

Cookie cutters come in various shapes and sizes and should be sharp enough to give a clean, precise outline. The top side will usually have a smooth, rounded edge to press down on, so make sure you use it the right way up. Choose metal cutters over plastic, if possible, for a neater finish. It is useful to have a graded set of plain or fluted metal cutters for everyday use, but you will find a selection of shapes available for special events or occasions.

COOKIE PRESS

A cookie press looks like an icing syringe and works by forcing the dough through a disc that shapes it into a simple pattern. Cookie presses work best for soft cookie doughs. Usually the press comes with a detailed recipe booklet.

SHORTBREAD MOLDS

The classic shortbread mold is traditionally engraved with a Scottish thistle motif and made of wood. You press the dough into the mold using your fingers and level off the surface with a palette knife. The dough should easily turn out from the mold when turned over onto a baking sheet.

PASTRY BRUSHES

Pastry brushes can be useful for brushing unbaked cookies with a milk or egg glaze, or brushing baked cookies with a sugar glaze. The best brushes should have bristles that are securely fixed into the handle. Bristles will be made of natural materials, nylon or even silicon, and will come in a range of shapes and sizes.

NOTE ON OVEN TEMPERATURES

Oven temperatures given in the recipes are for conventional ovens. If you have a fan-assisted oven, you will need to reduce the temperature accordingly, by 68°F (20°C). The cooking time will also need to be reduced, by about 20%. No preheating is usually necessary. Fan-assisted ovens all perform differently, so always refer to the manufacturer's instructions.

NOTE ON STORAGE

Cookies will keep for 5–7 days in an airtight container or can be frozen for up to 2 months, unless otherwise stated in a recipe.

Chocolate cookies

This chapter is for everyone who believes chocolate is a food group unto itself.

The sweet world is filled with myriad cookie lovers. Some are devoted to shortbread. Others can't see beyond oatmeal raisin. But most, we have to say, are hopelessly devoted to chocolate. This chapter is designed exclusively to satisfy their needs. Here you'll find everything from Chocolate peanut butter pinwheels (page 50) to Lemon and white chocolate cookies (page 29). All favorites are covered.

But within the chocolate cookie fan base is a group whose chocolate cravings are even more specific. We're talking about – you guessed it – the chocolate chip cookie lover.

The secret to a good chocolate chip cookie lies in the baking. Of course the recipe is important, but an over-cooked cookie is akin to an over-cooked fillet steak. It's edible, but it's just not the same. The science behind the cooking process is advanced, but the bottom line is simple: cookies continue to harden while cooling, so take them out of the oven while they are still slightly underdone. This advice can be applied to most cookies, so take heed. Soft and chewy, that's the key.

Condensed milk chocolate chip cookies

Ultimate

To me, these are the quintessential chocolate chip cookie. I know Lindsay would disagree, but we are from different ends of the world after all!

Makes 24

2 sticks (200g) **butter, softened**
scant ½ cup (75g) **extra-fine sugar**
½ cup (125ml) **sweetened condensed milk**
2¼ cups (250g) **all-purpose flour**
1 tsp **baking powder**
1¾ cups (300g) **chocolate chips or chunks**

Preheat the oven to 350°F/180°C. Line one or two baking sheets with baking parchment.

Beat the butter and sugar together in a large bowl until pale and creamy. Pour in the condensed milk and beat to combine. In a separate bowl combine the flour and baking powder. Stir into the butter mixture, then add the chocolate chips and mix to combine. Roll into tablespoon-sized balls and place on the prepared baking sheets. Press down gently with a fork and bake for 15–18 minutes, or until golden.

White chocolate and orange brownie cookies

Orange heaven

White chocolate and orange is a classic combination. These two flavors set in a brownie-type cookie make for an even better one.

Makes 24

1 stick (125g) **butter, softened**
1 cup (200g) **extra-fine sugar**
1 **egg**
Finely grated rind of 1 small orange
2 cups (225g) **all-purpose flour**
1 tsp **baking powder**
1 **pinch salt**
3 Tbsp **cocoa powder**
7oz (200g) **white chocolate,**
   cut into chunks

Preheat the oven to 350°F/180°C. Line a large baking sheet with baking parchment.

Cream the butter and sugar until pale. Add the egg and orange rind and beat to combine. In a separate bowl combine the flour, baking powder, salt and cocoa powder and add to the creamed mixture. Combine until a stiff mixture forms, then stir in the white chocolate until evenly dispersed. Roll the mixture into heaped tablespoon-sized balls and place on the prepared baking sheet, leaving a little space between the balls to allow for spreading.

Bake for 14–16 minutes, or until firm to the touch. Remove from the oven, transfer to a wire rack and allow to cool completely.

Lemon and white chocolate cookies

Lemon and white chocolate cookies

Fragrant

My very good friend Emily had cravings for lemon and white chocolate cookies when she was pregnant with her baby daughter Florence. I have tried to replicate the extortionately priced "organic" variety she used to buy from the local deli. Now you can eat twice as many, Em!

Makes 24–30

1 stick (125g) **butter,** softened
scant ¾ cup (125g) **extra-fine sugar**
1 tsp **pure lemon oil**
1 **egg**
4 cups (450g) **all-purpose flour**
1 tsp **baking powder**
2 Tbsp **milk**
10½oz (300g) **white chocolate**

Preheat the oven to 325°F/170°C. Line one or two baking sheets with baking parchment.

Beat the butter and sugar in a large bowl until pale and creamy. Add the lemon oil and beat for a further 30 seconds. Beat in the egg until just combined. In a separate bowl combine the flour and baking powder. Mix into the butter mixture, adding enough of the milk to make a dough.

Roll out the dough on a lightly floured surface, about ¼in (4mm) thick. Using a 2½-in (6-cm) round cutter, cut the dough into rounds then transfer onto the prepared trays.

Bake for 15–18 minutes, or until lightly golden. Allow to cool slightly, then transfer to a wire rack and allow to cool completely. When cool, melt the chocolate in the microwave or over a double boiler. Half dip the cookies into the chocolate, then leave to set on baking parchment in a cool place.

Anita's Afghans

Iced

Anita's Afghans are as much about the icing as the actual cookie. Anita, my very good friend, will whip up a batch for almost any occasion and they just seem to get better every time.

Makes 15

2 sticks (200g) **butter, softened**
¾ cup (150g) **extra-fine sugar**
2 cups (225g) **all-purpose flour**
½ cup (50g) **cocoa powder**
4 cups (75g) **cornflakes**
15 **walnut halves**

For the icing:
2 cups (300g) **confectioners sugar**
3 Tbsp **cocoa powder**
1 tsp **butter, softened**
3–4 Tbsp **water**

Preheat the oven to 400°F/200°C. Line a baking sheet with baking parchment.

Beat the butter and sugar in a large bowl until light and fluffy. In a separate bowl combine the flour and cocoa powder. Add to the butter mixture with the cornflakes and mix until combined. Shape the mixture into heaped tablespoon-sized balls and place on the baking sheet, leaving a little space between the cookies to allow for spreading. Flatten the balls slightly with your fingers.

Bake for 8 minutes. Turn off the oven and leave the cookies to sit for a further 5 minutes before removing them. Transfer to a wire rack and allow to cool completely.

When cool, prepare the icing. Sift the confectioners sugar and cocoa powder into a bowl. Add the soft butter and water and mix to form a stiff icing. Spoon a generous tablespoon of icing onto each cookie and top with a walnut half. Leave the icing to set before serving.

Chocolate and crystalized ginger cookies

Indulgent

I love a bit of crystalized ginger and chocolate as an after-dinner treat, although these cookies are good eaten at any time of day.

Makes 24

5½oz (150g) **unsweetened baking chocolate (70% cocoa solids)**
⅓ cup (75g) **butter,** softened
generous 1 cup (175g) **light brown sugar**
1 tsp **vanilla extract**
2 **egg yolks**
scant 1 cup (100g) **all-purpose flour**
½ cup (50g) **cocoa powder**
1 cup (150g) **crystalized ginger,** cut into chunks

Melt the chocolate in a heatproof bowl over a saucepan of simmering water or in the microwave. Set aside and allow to cool slightly.

Preheat the oven to 350°F/180°C. Line two baking sheets with baking parchment.

Beat the butter and sugar together in a large bowl until pale and creamy. Add the vanilla extract and egg yolks and beat to combine. In a separate bowl combine the flour and cocoa powder and sift into the butter mixture. Stir to combine, then add the melted chocolate and chopped ginger. Mix together. Shape the mixture into tablespoon-sized balls and place on the baking sheets, leaving a little space between them to allow for spreading. Press down with a fork and bake for 15–18 minutes or until softly set. Allow to cool for 5 minutes on the tray, then transfer to a wire rack and allow to cool completely.

These are best eaten the day they are made.

Chocolate coconut ganache cookies
Indulgent

These soft ganache-iced cookies are bittersweet and nutty. Serve them with coffee or tea and they won't be around for long!

Makes 20

½ cup (115g) **butter, softened**
¾ cup (115g) **light brown sugar**
1 **egg**
¾ cup (100g) **all-purpose flour**
¼ cup (25g) **cocoa powder**
1 tsp **baking powder**
1¼ cups (100g) **sweetened shredded coconut**

For the ganache:
3½oz (100g) **bittersweet chocolate, chopped**
¼ cup (60ml) **heavy cream**
1 Tbsp **butter**

Coconut shavings

Preheat the oven to 350°F/180°C. Line two baking sheets with baking parchment.

Beat the butter and sugar together until pale and creamy. Beat in the egg, then sift in the flour, cocoa powder and baking powder. Mix to combine, then stir in the coconut. Roll the mixture into tablespoon-sized balls and place on the prepared baking sheets, leaving enough room between them to allow for spreading. Dip your thumb in flour and press a deep hole in the center of each ball, flattening them out slightly.

Bake for 10–12 minutes or until cooked. Press the indentation again with your finger to enhance the hollow. Allow to cool for 2 minutes on the baking sheets before transferring to a wire rack.

When cool, make the ganache. Place the chopped chocolate in a medium-sized bowl. Set aside. Heat the cream and butter in a small saucepan over medium heat. Bring just to a boil. Immediately pour the boiling cream over the chocolate and allow to stand for 5 minutes. Stir with a whisk until smooth. Spoon the chocolate ganache into the hollowed part of the cookie and top with a couple of shreds of coconut. Store in a single layer in an airtight container.

Chocolate coconut ganache cookies

Chocolate salami

Chocolate salami

Rich

This chocolate and cookie mixture in the shape of a salami makes a great gift. Slice it thinly and serve with coffee.

Makes 1 log

9oz (250g) **graham crackers**
1¼ cups (200g) **roasted Brazil nuts**
7oz (200g) **unsweetened baking
    chocolate (70% cocoa solids)**
1½ sticks (175g) **butter**
Grated rind of 1 **orange**
1 Tbsp **Cointreau or brandy**

In a food processor finely grind the crackers. Add the Brazil nuts and pulse three or four times until chopped but still chunky.

In a small saucepan heat the chocolate and butter until just melted. Remove from the heat and stir in the orange rind and Cointreau or brandy. Stir into the cracker mixture until well combined. Put in the fridge for about 2 hours, or until cool and beginning to set.

Lay a large piece of baking parchment (about 18in/45cm long) out on a flat surface. Using your hands, tip the mixture onto the paper and manipulate into a sausage shape about 12in (30cm) long and 1½in–2in (4–5cm) in diameter. Roll tightly, securing the ends, and refrigerate overnight or until set. Remove from the fridge 45 minutes to 1 hour before slicing and serving.

This can be kept in the fridge for up to 3 weeks – a great festive season standby.

Chocolate and sour cherry truffle cookies

Sweet-sour

The sharpness of the sour cherries breaks through the sweet cookies – a perfect balance.

Makes 20–24

¾ cup (100g) **all-purpose flour**
½ cup (50g) **cocoa powder**
1 tsp **baking powder**
scant 1 cup (175g) **extra-fine sugar**
½ stick (50g) **butter, softened and cut into cubes**
2 **eggs,** beaten
1 tsp **vanilla extract**
generous ½ cup (100g) **dried sour cherries**
¾ cup (100g) **confectioners sugar**

Sift the flour, cocoa powder and baking powder into a large bowl. Add the sugar and stir to combine. Rub in the butter until the mixture resembles fine breadcrumbs. Add the beaten eggs and vanilla and stir in, together with the sour cherries. Cover with plastic wrap and chill the mixture for at least 30 minutes.

Preheat the oven to 400°F/200°C and line a baking sheet with baking parchment.

Roll the mixture into tablespoon-sized balls and drop into the confectioners sugar. (You won't be able to roll perfectly shaped balls as the mixture is still sticky!) Shake well until coated in a thick layer of confectioners sugar. Transfer to a baking sheet and bake for 10 minutes or until just set. Transfer to a wire rack and allow to cool completely.

Pecan chocolate chip clusters

Velvety

The chocolate chip cookie in a shortbread, melt-in-your-mouth form.

Makes 30–35

1½ cups (330g) **butter,** softened
½ tsp **salt**
scant 1 cup (125g) **confectioners
sugar**
1 tsp **rum extract**
1 tsp **cold water**
4 cups (450g) **all-purpose flour,**
such as pastry flour or 00 flour
(see page 14)
1¼ cups (130g) **pecan nuts,** chopped
and toasted
1½ cups (300g) **plain chocolate chips
or plain chocolate,** chopped

Cream the butter and salt in an electric mixer until pale and smooth. Gradually add the confectioners sugar and cream until light and fluffy, about 5 minutes. Beat in the rum extract and cold water. In a separate bowl combine the flour, pecan nuts and chocolate. Add to the butter mixture and stir until combined. Cover and refrigerate the dough for 30 minutes.

Preheat the oven to 325°F/160°C.

Shape the dough into rounded teaspoon-sized balls and place, 2in (5cm) apart, on ungreased baking sheets. Bake for 20–25 minutes, until the edges are slightly golden. Allow to cool for 5 minutes on the baking sheets, then transfer to wire racks and allow to cool completely.

White chocolate and macadamia cookies
Chunky

This is one of the most tempting cookie combinations ever.

Makes 20

1 stick (125g) **butter,** softened
1½ cups (225g) **soft brown sugar**
1 **egg,** lightly beaten
1 tsp **vanilla extract**
2 cups (225g) **all-purpose flour**
½ tsp **baking powder**
1 **pinch salt**
generous 1 cup (200g) **white chocolate chunks or chips**
1¼ cups (150g) **macadamia nuts, roughly chopped**

Preheat the oven to 350°F/180°C. Line a baking sheet with baking parchment.

Beat the butter and sugar together in a large bowl until pale and creamy. Add the egg and vanilla extract and stir to combine. Combine the flour, baking powder and salt together in a separate bowl and stir into the butter mixture until just combined. Fold through the chocolate chunks and macadamia nuts.

Place heaped tablespoonfuls of the mixture onto the prepared baking sheet, leaving a little space between them to allow for spreading.

Bake for 15–20 minutes, or until lightly golden. Allow to cool on the sheets for 5 minutes, then transfer to a wire rack and allow to cool completely.

White chocolate and macadamia cookies

Chocolate truffle cookies

Chocolate truffle cookies

Silky

The slightly crispy exterior of these incredible little cookies engulfs the silky smooth "truffle" within. Use the best unsweetened baking chocolate you can find – the better the chocolate, the better the truffle!

Makes 40–42

9oz (250g) **unsweetened baking chocolate (70% cocoa solids), broken**
generous ½ cup (60g) **cocoa powder, sifted**
1 stick (110g) **butter**
3 **eggs**
1 cup (200g) **extra-fine sugar**
1½ tsp **vanilla extract**
⅔ cup (75g) **all-purpose flour**
¼ tsp **baking powder**
¼ tsp **salt**
5½oz (150g) **unsweetened baking chocolate (70% cocoa solids), chopped into small chunks**

Preheat the oven to 350°F/180°C.

Combine the broken chocolate pieces, the cocoa powder and butter in a metal bowl and place over a pan of simmering water. Stir occasionally until the chocolate and butter have melted.

Remove from the heat, stir to combine and set aside to cool.

Beat the eggs and sugar, using an electric mixer, until light and fluffy. Beat in the vanilla extract and chocolate mixture. Sift together the flour, baking powder and salt. Add to the butter mixture together with the chopped chocolate and stir until just combined.

Cover the dough and chill for at least 3 hours. Even after chilling, the dough will be quite soft. Quickly roll the dough into heaped teaspoon-sized balls (roughly 1in/3cm wide) and place 2in (5cm) apart on ungreased or parchment-lined baking sheets. Bake for 10 minutes, or until the tops are crispy and the centers just set.

Allow to cool for 5 minutes on the baking sheets, then transfer to a wire rack and allow to cool completely. Dust with cocoa powder to serve.

The classic chocolate chip cookie
Classic

What you'll find here is a simple round cookie, slightly crisp on the outside, chewy on the inside and studded with plenty of chocolate chips. If you can't find good-quality chocolate chips, use good-quality chocolate, and chop it up into chip-sized chunks. Either way, you'll get your chocolate chip cookie fix!

Makes 26–28 large cookies

2¼ sticks (220g) **butter**
1 cup (160g) **brown sugar**
generous ½ cup (110g) **extra-fine sugar**
2 **eggs**
1 tsp **vanilla extract**
2¾ cups (300g) **all-purpose flour**
1 tsp **baking soda**
½ tsp **salt**
1½ cups (250g) **chocolate chips or bittersweet chocolate,** chopped

Preheat the oven to 375°F/190°C.

Beat the butter and sugars together until smooth. Add the eggs and vanilla and continue beating until combined. Sift the flour, baking soda and salt together and stir into the butter mixture until just combined. Add the chocolate chips or chopped chocolate and stir until incorporated.

Drop rounded tablespoonfuls of the dough onto ungreased baking sheets, about 2in (5cm) apart. Bake for 10–12 minutes, until the surface is just set but the centers are still soft. They will appear underdone, but will continue to harden while cooling. The secret is to NOT over-cook them!

Allow to cool on the baking sheets for 2 minutes (no longer or they may harden too much), then transfer to wire racks and allow to cool completely.

Store in an airtight container for up to 5 days, but I've never know them to last that long!

Double chocolate cookies

Rich

These delectable cookies made an appearance in our second book, *Ice Cream!*, where we sandwiched fresh mint ice cream between them. Enjoy them whichever way you like!

Makes 30

2 sticks (200g) **butter**
1¼ cups (250g) **extra-fine sugar**
¾ cup (125g) **light brown sugar**
1 **egg**
1 tsp **vanilla extract**
1½oz (45g) **cocoa powder**
2 Tbsp **milk**
2¼ cups (250g) **all-purpose flour**
¾ tsp **baking soda**
5½oz (150g) **bittersweet or white chocolate**, chopped

Preheat the oven to 350°F/180°C. Line two baking sheets with baking parchment.

Cream the butter and sugars together until light and fluffy. Beat in the egg and vanilla extract, then the cocoa powder and milk. Sift the flour and baking soda together and stir into the butter mixture until just blended. Stir in the chopped chocolate.

Shape the dough into rounded tablespoon-sized balls and place 2in (5cm) apart on the baking sheets. Bake for 12 minutes, allow to cool on the baking sheets for a few minutes, then transfer to a wire rack and allow to cool completely.

Store in an airtight container for up to 5 days.

Chocolate chip slab cookies
Addictive

These cookies go hand in hand with Wilson family sailing trips, road trips, lazy afternoons at the lake and cozy après-ski winter days. They are a decadent, yet simple, family staple. All thanks go to the Canadian cookbook series *Best of Bridge* for allowing us to include the recipe in this book.

Makes 12–18 large squares

scant 1 cup (220g) **butter, softened**
1¼ cups (200g) **brown sugar**
1 tsp **vanilla extract**
2½ cups (300g) **all-purpose flour**
7oz (200g) **bittersweet or milk chocolate chips or bittersweet or milk chocolate,** chopped into chunks

Preheat the oven to 350°F/180°C. Line the base of a 7 x 10¾-in (18 x 27-cm) baking pan.

Beat the butter and sugar using an electric mixer until light and fluffy, about 5 minutes (the secret!). Beat in the vanilla extract. Stir in the flour and chocolate chips. Pat the dough into the prepared baking tray. Bake for 25–28 minutes, until the edges are slightly crispy. Allow to cool before cutting into squares.

Chocolate chip slab cookies

Chocolate chip oatmeal cookies

Chocolate chip oatmeal cookies

Moreish

Crispy on the outside, chewy on the inside, packed with chocolate, slightly sweet and always the first to disappear from the cookie jar. What more can we say?

Makes approx. 24

¼ cup (60ml) **vegetable oil**
⅓ cup (75g) **butter, softened**
½ cup (100g) **extra-fine sugar**
¾ cup (110g) **light brown sugar**
½ tsp **vanilla extract**
1 **egg**
1 cup (100g) **dry quick oatmeal**
scant 1½ cups (150g) **all-purpose flour**
½ tsp **baking soda**
½ tsp **baking powder**
pinch **salt**
1 cup (150g) **bittersweet chocolate chips or bittersweet chocolate, chopped**

Preheat the oven to 350°F/180°C.

Combine the oil, butter and sugars in a large mixing bowl and cream until smooth. Beat in the vanilla and eggs, one at a time, then stir in the oats. In a separate bowl, sift the flour with the baking soda, baking powder and salt. Using a wooden spoon, stir the flour mixture into the buttery oat mixture together with the chocolate chips. Stir until just combined.

Drop rounded tablespoonfuls of the dough, 2in (5cm) apart, onto ungreased baking sheets. Bake for 10 minutes, until the surface is set and the centers slightly soft. Allow to cool on the baking sheets for 5 minutes, then transfer to wire racks and allow to cool completely. The cookies will firm up slightly while cooling, so don't over-cook.

Chocolate and pepper cookies

Sharp

A touch of black pepper and a pinch of cayenne add a mysterious edge to these cookies. Pepper, however, doesn't shift them into savory territory. They are still a sweet cookie, perfect with espresso or a cup of tea.

Makes 30

scant 1 cup (220g) **butter, softened**
¾ cup (100g) **confectioners sugar**
1 tsp **vanilla extract**
scant 2 cups (220g) **all-purpose flour**
scant ½ cup (50g) **cocoa powder**
½ tsp **freshly ground black pepper**
⅛ tsp **cayenne**
2–3 Tbsp **demerara sugar, for rolling**
 (see page 12)

Cream the butter and confectioners sugar for 3–4 minutes, using an electric mixer, until light and fluffy. Add the vanilla extract and beat until smooth. Sift the flour, cocoa powder, pepper and cayenne together. Add to the butter mixture and stir until smooth. Tip the dough onto a work surface and shape into a 6-in (15-cm) long log.

Roll the log in demerara sugar, pressing gently so the sugar will adhere. Cover with plastic wrap and chill for 1 hour.

Preheat the oven to 350°F/180°C. Line two baking sheets with baking parchment, or lightly grease.

Slice the log into ¼-in (5-mm) thick slices. Place on the lined or greased baking sheets and bake for 12–15 minutes, until set. Allow to cool on the baking sheets for 5 minutes, then transfer to wire racks and allow to cool completely.

Store in an airtight container for up to 5 days. Alternatively, tightly wrap the dough in plastic wrap and freeze for up to 1 month. Defrost in the refrigerator before slicing and baking.

Frogs

Fast

These chewy little delights, made quickly in a saucepan, have many names. Haystacks, frogs, no-bake cookies … regardless of what you decide to call them, they will undoubtedly become a favorite.

Makes approx. 35

2 cups (400g) **granulated sugar**
1 stick (110g) **butter**
generous ½ cup (60g) **cocoa powder,** sifted
½ cup (125ml) **milk**
½ tsp **vanilla extract**
⅛ tsp **salt**
generous 1¼ cups (150g) **dry quick oatmeal**
1¼ cups (100g) **unsweetened shredded coconut**

Line two baking sheets with wax paper or baking parchment.

Combine the sugar, butter and cocoa powder and milk in a saucepan over medium heat. Bring the mixture to a boil, whisking occasionally to remove any lumps. Reduce the heat to medium-low and boil gently for 5 minutes. Remove the saucepan from heat and stir in the vanilla extract and salt. Add the oats and coconut and stir to combine.

Spoon rounded tablespoonfuls of the mixture onto lined trays. Chill for at least 1 hour.

Peel the "frogs" from the paper and store in an airtight container in the fridge for up to 5 days.

Chocolate peanut butter pinwheels

Impressive

I found this recipe in my grandmother's Christmas recipe collection. The pinwheels made an appearance on her Christmas cookie tray throughout the '50s, '60s and '70s. Somehow they fell by the wayside but now, thanks to Christmas-time recipe testing, they are back!

Makes 48

½ cup (125g) **butter**
1½ cups (220g) **extra-fine sugar**
½ cup (125g) **creamy peanut butter**
1 **egg,** lightly beaten
2 Tbsp **milk**
2½ cups (275g) **all-purpose flour**
½ tsp **salt**
½ tsp **baking soda**
6oz (175g) **unsweetened baking chocolate,** broken
1 tsp **butter**

Combine the butter, sugar and peanut butter in a large mixing bowl and beat with an electric whisk until smooth and creamy. Add the egg and milk and beat until smooth. In a separate bowl sift the flour, salt and baking soda together. Add to the butter mixture and, using a wooden spoon, stir until just combined. Cover and refrigerate for 1 hour.

Combine the chocolate and 1 tsp butter in a saucepan over low heat and stir until melted. Set aside.

Divide the dough into two equal parts and shape into balls. Flour a work surface and roll one ball into a 9½ x 12-in (24 x 30-cm) rectangle, ¼in (5mm) thick. Spread half of the chocolate mixture over the rectangle. Starting at a narrow end, carefully roll up the dough to the other end. Continue with the other roll. Place both rolls, seam-side down, on a parchment-lined baking sheet and chill for 20 minutes.

Preheat the oven to 400°F/200°C.

Transfer the rolls to a floured surface and slice into ½-in (1-cm) wide cookies. Place on parchment-lined baking sheets and bake for 8–10 minutes, until set and slightly golden. Allow to cool for 5 minutes on the baking sheets, then transfer to wire racks and allow to cool completely.

Chocolate peanut butter pinwheels

Bars and oat cookies

Bars, slices, squares. Whatever you call them, they describe the world of flat cookies bordered by a baking pan. Some are simple one-layer cookies, like a brownie or a muesli bar. Others are two layer-cookies, made in two steps. This is where our Pecan and caramel bar (page 71) comes in. Some bars reach the three-level height. Bring on the Nanaimo bar (see the recipe for the origins of that one, page 73). All can be sliced according to personal whim. Neatness can be achieved by trimming the sides before cutting the bars into squares or rectangles. Whole rows can be devoured. We like to say we're just making it even.

Sometimes bars, slices or squares can be healthy. That's how oat cookies wiggled their way into this chapter. Oats suggest healthy, right? There are, after all, oat cookies that feature carob and soy. But recipes like these just didn't make the grade. In fact, they triggered quite a debate among our tasters. Should a cookie be healthy in the first place? Some said no. If it's something healthy you want, have a piece of fruit. Others said if you can't tell it's healthy, then why not include it?

Our bottom line is simple – if it tastes delicious, it makes the grade. We don't believe in abstinence.

Apricot muesli bars

Tasty

This is adapted from a recipe I developed when I used to work in the Nestlé test kitchens many years ago. As you can imagine, chocolate was in abundance.

Makes 16–20 bars

scant 1 cup (50g) **dried apricots,** **chopped into quarters**
½ cup (125ml) **water**
scant 1½ sticks (150g) **butter,** **softened**
generous 1 cup (175g) **light brown** **sugar**
scant 1½ cups (150g) **all-purpose** **flour**
1 tsp **baking powder**
1 cup (100g) **dry quick oatmeal**
3½oz (100g) **bittersweet, milk or** **white chocolate, finely chopped**

Preheat the oven to 325°F/170°C. Line the base of a 10¾ x 7 x 1¼-in (27 x 18 x 3-cm) shallow baking pan with baking parchment.

Put the apricots and water in a small saucepan. Bring to a boil, reduce the heat and simmer until all the liquid has been absorbed. Remove from the heat and stir in the butter until melted. Add the sugar, stir to combine and allow to cool.

Combine the flour and baking powder and add to the cooled mixture with the oats and chocolate. Press into the pan and bake for 30–35 minutes, or until a skewer inserted comes out clean. Allow to cool in the pan for about 10 minutes then turn out onto a wire rack and allow to cool completely. Cut into bars or squares to serve.

Pecan and ginger oatcakes

Chunky

These are not for the sweet-toothed but they are delicious and make a great snack for kids with a glass of milk on the side.

Makes 15–18

½ cup (150g) **unsalted butter,**
   softened
scant 1½ cups (75g) **extra-fine sugar**
1 **large egg**
scant 1 cup (100g) **pecan nuts,**
   roughly chopped
2 **pieces preserved ginger** (about
   1½–1¾oz/40–50g)
1 cup (125g) **all-purpose flour**
¾ cup (75g) **dry quick oatmeal**
1 pinch **salt**
2 Tbsp **demerara sugar** (see
   page 12)

Preheat the oven to 350°F/180°C. Grease or line a large baking sheet.

Cream the butter and sugar until pale, then beat in the egg. Fold in the nuts, ginger, flour, oats and salt. Drop heaped tablespoonfuls of the mixture onto the baking sheet and gently flatten to approximately ½in (1cm) thick. Sprinkle the sugar over the cookies and bake for 15–18 minutes, or until golden around the edges and lightly golden on top. Transfer to a wire rack and allow to cool completely.

Anakiwa flapjacks

Substantial

This recipe is based on the energy-giving bars I became very addicted to when I did Outward Bound in Anakiwa, New Zealand. In North America, a flapjack refers to a thick pancake cooked on a griddle – so don't be confused.

Makes 8–16

½ cup (125g) **butter**
¼ cup (75ml) **corn syrup**
1 tsp **baking soda**
1 Tbsp **water**
¾ cup (75g) **dry quick oatmeal**
½ cup (75g) **yellow raisins**
1¼ cups (150g) **all-purpose flour**
½ cup (75g) **sunflower seeds,** roasted for 8–10 minutes at 350°F/180°C
¾ cup (50g) **sweetened shredded coconut**
¾ cup (100g) **demerara sugar** (see page 12)
scant 1 cup (150g) **dried apricots,** chopped

Preheat the oven to 325°F/170°C. Line the base and sides of a 10¾ x 7-in (27 x 18-cm) shallow baking pan.

Put the butter and corn syrup in a saucepan over low heat until the butter has melted. Dissolve the baking soda in 1 Tbsp boiling water and add to the butter mixture. Stir until the mixture foams then set aside.

In a large bowl combine all the remaining ingredients. Pour over the baking soda mixture and stir well until all the dry ingredients are combined. Tip the mixture into the prepared baking pan and press down firmly. Bake for about 30 minutes, or until golden and firm to touch. Allow to cool in the pan before cutting into bars.

Anakiwa flapjacks

White chocolate, cranberry and oat cookies
Balanced

Sweet chocolate, sharp cranberries and savory oats make for a blissful combination.

Makes 24–30

2 sticks (200g) **butter, softened**
generous 1¼ cups (200g) **light brown muscovado sugar** (see page 12)
½ cup (125ml) **sweetened condensed milk**
1 **large egg**
1 tsp **vanilla extract**
1⅔ cups (200g) **all-purpose flour**
½ tsp **baking soda**
1½ cups (150g) **dry quick oatmeal**
1 cup (150g) **dried cranberries**
generous ½ cup (100g) **white chocolate chips**

Preheat the oven to 325°F/160°C. Grease two baking sheets or line with baking parchment.

Cream the butter and sugar in a medium bowl until pale and smooth. Add the condensed milk, egg and vanilla extract and beat to combine until light and fluffy.

Combine the flour and baking soda together and stir into the creamed mixture. Stir in the oats, cranberries and chocolate chips. Place heaped tablespoonfuls of the mixture onto the prepared baking sheets, leaving a little space between them to allow for spreading, and press them down gently with a fork.

Bake for 15–18 minutes, or until golden brown. Allow to cool for 5 minutes on the baking sheet, then transfer to a wire rack and allow to cool completely.

Dream bars

Simplicity

So-called because you can choose your favorite toppings and it will work every time!

Makes 16–20

3 cups (175g) **graham cracker crumbs**
⅓ cup (75g) **butter,** melted
scant 1 cup (150g) **chocolate chunks or chips**
1 cup (150g) **dates,** chopped
½ cup (75g) **dried apricots,** chopped
½ cup (50g) **sweetened shredded coconut**
½ cup (50g) **flaked almonds**
1 x 14-oz (397-g) can **sweetened condensed milk**

Preheat the oven to 350°F/180°C. Line the base of an 7 x 10 ¾-in (18 x 27-cm) shallow baking pan with baking parchment.

Combine the cracker crumbs and melted butter and pour into the pan. Press into the pan, using the back of a spoon, until even and smooth. Sprinkle the chocolate, dates, apricots and coconut evenly over the base. Top with the flaked almonds, then evenly drizzle over the condensed milk.

Bake in the oven for 25–30 minutes, or until golden on top. Allow to cool in the pan, then slice into squares or bars before eating.

Ginger crunch

Ginger crunch

Delectable

This extra thick ginger slice is my nemesis. A perfect accompaniment to a good creamy coffee!

Makes 16–24

For the base:
2 cups (225g) **all-purpose flour**
½ cup (100g) **extra-fine sugar**
1 tsp **baking powder**
2 tsp **ground ginger**
½ cup (150g) **butter, cut into cubes**

For the icing:
½ cup (150g) **butter**
¼ cup (60ml) **corn syrup**
2 cups (300g) **confectioners sugar, sifted**
2 Tbsp **ground ginger**

Preheat the oven to 350°F/180°C. Line a deep-sided 7 x 10¾-in (18 x 27-cm) shallow baking pan with baking parchment.

To make the base, put the flour, sugar, baking powder and ginger in a food processor. Pulse several times to combine, then add the butter. Process for about 30 seconds, or until the mixture resembles fine breadcrumbs. Press the mixture evenly into the pan and level off, using the back of a spoon.

Bake for 20–25 minutes, or until lightly golden. Remove from the oven and allow to cool completely.

To make the icing, put the butter and corn syrup in a medium saucepan and heat until just melted. Add the sifted confectioners sugar and ginger and cook for a further 1–2 minutes, stirring constantly until smooth. Remove from the heat and pour over the base. Leave to set. Remove from the pan and cut into squares or triangles to serve.

Date and hazelnut crumble slice

Textured

This one's for Mom. It makes a good substitute for dessert when served with a generous dollop of crème fraîche or yogurt and is equally good for morning or afternoon snack.

Makes 8–16

For the filling:
2½ cups (400g) **dried pitted dates,** roughly chopped
Grated rind of 2 **lemons**
generous 1 cup (250ml) **water**
½ cup (75g) **sugar**

For the base:
2 cups (225g) **all-purpose flour**
½ cup (100g) **extra-fine sugar**
1 tsp **baking powder**
1 stick (125g) **firm butter,** cut into chunks

For the crumble topping:
scant 1 cup (100g) **all-purpose flour**
generous ½ cup (50g) **light brown sugar**
scant ½ cup (75g) **hazelnuts,** roughly chopped
⅓ cup (75g) **firm butter**

Preheat the oven to 400°F/200°C and line an 7 x 10 ¾-in (18 x 27-cm) baking pan with baking parchment.

Put the filling ingredients in a saucepan and bring to a boil. Reduce the heat and simmer for 10–15 minutes, or until thick. Allow to cool.

Mix together the flour, extra-fine sugar and baking powder for the base. Using your hands or a food processor, rub in the butter to resemble fine breadcrumbs. Press the mixture firmly into the pan and bake for 15–18 minutes, or until brown around the edges. Remove from the oven.

Combine the crumble ingredients together in another bowl until the mixture is crumbly. Spread the date mixture over the cooked base, then sprinkle over the crumble mixture, pressing it down firmly but gently. Return to the oven and cook for a further 15–20 minutes, or until the crumble topping is golden. Allow to cool completely in the pan before serving or serve warm with a spoonful of vanilla ice cream.

Date and hazelnut crumble slice

Lemon and blueberry shortcake slice

Lemon and blueberry shortcake slice

Paradise

These have a gooey, lemon curd-like center with a crispy meringue-like crust. Delicious, and our photographer Stuart's favorite!

Makes 16–20

For the base:
2 cups (225g) **all-purpose flour**
½ cup (100g) **extra-fine sugar**
1½ sticks (175g) **firm butter,** cut into cubes

For the topping:
3 **eggs**
generous 1 cup (225g) **extra-fine sugar,** for the base
Juice (about ½ cup/100ml) **and** grated **rind of** 3 **lemons**
⅓ cup (40g) **flour**
½ cup (75g) **dried blueberries** (optional)
Confectioners sugar, to serve (optional)

Preheat the oven to 350°F/180°C. Line the base and sides of an 7 x 10¾-in (18 x 27-cm) pan with baking parchment.

Put the flour and the first measure of sugar in a large bowl or food processor and mix to combine. Add the butter and rub together or process until the mixture resembles fine breadcrumbs. Press the crumbs evenly into the prepared pan and bake for 20–25 minutes, or until golden. Remove and reduce the temperature to 275°F/140°C.

While the base is cooking, whisk together the eggs and the second measure of sugar, using an electric mixer, until very thick and pale, about 8–10 minutes. Stir in the lemon juice and rind, then fold in the flour. Sprinkle the blueberries evenly over the base, if using. Pour over the egg mixture and bake for 35–40 minutes, or until set. Allow to cool in the pan before cutting into bars. Serve dusted with confectioners sugar, if liked.

■ *Try stirring fresh blueberries into the lemon topping before baking, instead of dried.*

Coconut and jam slice

Sticky

This slice is often referred to as Louise cake – but who's Louise? I've kept its name simple so you know exactly what you're getting. It is loved by young and old alike.

Makes approx. 20 triangles

For the base:
scant 1 cup (175g) **extra-fine sugar**
1 stick (115g) **butter,** softened
2 **eggs,** separated
½ tsp **vanilla extract**
2 cups (225g) **all-purpose flour**
1 tsp **baking powder**

For the topping:
⅔ cup (150g) **raspberry jam**
½ cup (100g) **extra-fine sugar**
¾ cup (40g) **sweetened shredded coconut**

Preheat the oven to 325°F/160°C. Line the base of a 7 x 10¾-in (18 x 27-cm) baking pan with baking parchment and set aside.

To make the base, beat the sugar and butter until creamy and pale. Beat in the egg yolks and vanilla extract, then add the flour and baking powder. Combine together to form a stiff mixture and press into the prepared pan. Spread the raw base with the raspberry jam. Using clean beaters, beat the egg whites until soft peaks form, then beat in the second measure of sugar and continue beating until the mixture forms a glossy meringue. Fold in the coconut and spread evenly over the jam and base.

Bake for about 1 hour, or until crisp and golden. Cut the slice into triangles while still warm.

Energizing muesli bars
Sweet fuel

These bars straddle the fence between a tasty, energy bar packed with treats and goodness, and a decadent bar worthy of dessert status. Either way, the inspiration for this recipe is thanks to family friend and fine baker Sandra Nowlan.

Makes approx. 25 squares

1 stick (110g) **butter**, melted
generous ½ cup (80g) **light brown sugar**
¼ cup (80ml) **corn syrup**
3 heaped Tbsp **creamy peanut butter**
2 cups (200g) **dry quick oatmeal**
½ cup (60g) **wheatgerm**
¾ cup (50g) **unsweetened shredded coconut**
5½oz (150g) **chocolate**, finely chopped or chocolate chips
generous ¼ cup (40g) **Rice Krispies®**
generous ¼ cup (40g) **sunflower seeds (see tip)**

Preheat the oven to 350°F/180°C.

In a medium-sized bowl stir together the melted butter, brown sugar, corn syrup and peanut butter until smooth. Combine the remaining ingredients together in a separate bowl. Add the peanut butter mixture and mix well until combined.

Press the mixture into a greased 9-in (23-cm) square pan. Bake for 25 minutes, or until the top is golden. Allow to cool, then cut into bars.

■ *Chopped nuts can replace the sunflower seeds.*

Nova Scotian seed oatcakes

Wholesome

Oatcakes, traditionally a savory Scottish cookie, have evolved into something quite unique on Canada's East Coast. Here is our take on the Nova Scotian oatcake – a version of family friend's Sandra Nowlan's delicious thick, cookie-cake-like recipe combined with a handful of health-giving seeds.

Makes 20–22

2 cups (450g) **butter,** softened
1 cup (200g) **extra-fine sugar**
2½ cups (300g) **all-purpose flour**
1¼ cups (150g) **whole wheat flour**
¼ tsp **salt**
1 Tbsp **each flax, poppy and sesame seeds,** toasted
2 Tbsp **cold water**
2¾ cups (300g) **dry quick oatmeal**

Preheat the oven to 375°F/190°C.

In a large bowl cream the butter and sugar together until smooth. In a separate bowl, sift the flours with the salt. Add to the butter mixture with the toasted seeds and water. Stir to combine.

Lightly flour a work surface and tip the oats on top. Gather the dough into a mound and place on top of the oats.

Gently knead the dough into the oats, gathering any oats that scatter away and placing them back into the dough. When the oats are combined, divide the dough into two portions, setting one aside. Shape into a ball and roll into a circle roughly ⅝in (1.5cm) thick. Make sure the circle is of even thickness throughout. Using an 3¼-in (8-cm) wide cookie cutter or drinking glass, cut out oatcakes and place them on an ungreased or parchment-lined baking sheet. Re-shape the extra dough (so it is of similar thickness) and cut oatcakes until all dough is used. Continue with the remaining portion of dough.

Bake for 20–25 minutes, until the edges are just golden but the centers still slightly soft. Allow to cool on the baking sheet for 5 minutes, then transfer to wire racks and allow to cool completely.

Nova Scotian seed oatcakes

Pecan and caramel bars

Pecan and caramel bars

Decadent

Let's face it – baking may make you happy, but the accolades received do satisfy our inner show-off needs. This is where these bars come in. And what's better? Pure deliciousness doesn't get much easier.

Makes 20

For the base:
2½ cups (300g) **all-purpose flour**
½ cup (150g) **soft brown sugar**
½ cup (150g) **butter,** cut into cubes
1¾ cups (200g) **pecan nuts**

For the topping:
1½ sticks (175g) **butter**
¾ cup (80g) **soft brown sugar**

Preheat the oven to 350°F/180°C.

To make the base, combine the flour, brown sugar and butter in a large bowl and blend with a fork until crumbly. Pat the mixture into a 9 x13-in (23 x 33-cm) baking pan. Sprinkle the pecan nuts on top and set aside.

Make the topping. In a saucepan combine the butter and brown sugar over medium heat. Bring to a boil and stir constantly for 1 minute. Pour the caramel mixture over the pecan-covered base.

Bake for 18–20 minutes, until the caramel bubbles and the crust is golden. Allow the pan to cool on wire racks before cutting the bars into roughly 1½in x 3¼in (4 x 8-cm) servings.

Store the bars in an airtight container for 3–5 days.

Hello Dolly's
Divine

Who knows why these divine inventions are called Hello Dolly's. Perhaps it's because when the first bite was taken, all the recipient could say was, "Hello Dolly!" They are just that good. And when something is that good, who really cares who Dolly was anyway?

Makes 25 x 1½-in (4-cm) squares

1 stick (125ml) **butter,** melted
5½oz (150g) **graham crackers or oatmeal cookies,** crushed to crumbs
1½ cups (80g) **unsweetened shredded coconut**
generous ½ cup (75g) **pecan nuts,** chopped
5½oz (150g) **chocolate chips or chocolate,** finely chopped
generous 1 cup (250ml) **sweetened condensed milk**

Preheat the oven to 325°F/160°C.

In a medium-sized bowl combine the melted butter and cracker crumbs. Pat into a 8 x 8-in (20 x 20-cm) square pan. Cover with coconut, pecan nuts and chocolate. Finish with a drizzled layer of condensed milk.

Bake for 35 minutes, until the edges are golden. Allow to cool, then cut into squares.

Nanaimo bars

Rich

Nanaimo bars are a Canadian favorite. Legend has it that the first recipe was printed in the 1952 *Nanaimo Hospital Cookbook*, submitted by the Women's Auxiliary of Nanaimo, British Columbia. Thanks go to Aunt Susan's recipe archives for her version of our national staple.

Makes 40 squares

For the base:
scant 1 cup (220g) **butter**
2 Tbsp **extra-fine sugar**
2 **eggs,** lightly beaten
3 cups (200g) **unsweetened shredded coconut**
12oz (350g) **chocolate-covered graham crackers,** crushed to crumbs

For the filling:
½ stick (70g) **butter,** melted
¼ cup (75ml) **milk**
1 tsp **vanilla extract**
3½ cups (500g) **confectioners sugar**
2 Tbsp **instant vanilla pudding powder or custard mix**

For the topping:
7oz (200g) **unsweetened baking chocolate**
2 Tbsp **butter**

Preheat the oven to 350°F/180°C. Lightly grease a 9 x 13-in (23 x 33-cm) baking pan.

Combine butter, sugar and eggs in a bowl and whisk until smooth. Add coconut and cracker crumbs and stir to combine. Press mixture into pan and bake until firm, about 20 minutes. Allow to cool completely on a wire rack.

Combine all the filling ingredients in a mixing bowl and beat until creamy. Spread over the base and chill for 30 minutes in the refrigerator.

For the topping, combine the chocolate and butter in a metal bowl, suspended over a saucepan of simmering water. Stir occasionally until smooth. Spread chocolate mixture over the filling and return the pan to the refrigerator to chill until the topping has hardened. The squares will keep in the fridge for up to 7 days.

■ *For a St. Patrick's Day variation (or a treat at any time of the year), add a few drops of peppermint extract and green food coloring to the creamy middle layer and stir until uniform in color.*

Coconut marshmallows

Delicate

These cloud-like, heavenly marshmallows are more squares than bars, and more sweet treats than cookies, but we've put them in the book due to popular demand. Allow one day of resting time when making these marshmallows.

Makes approx. 40 squares

2½ cups (300g) **sweetened shredded coconut**
4 packets **unflavored gelatin**
(about 4 Tbsp)
1¼ cups (300ml) **water**
2¾ cups (600g) **extra-fine sugar**
1¼ cups (280ml) **corn syrup**
¼ tsp **salt**
1 tsp **coconut extract**

Preheat the oven to 325°F/160°C.

Spread the coconut evenly over a baking sheet and toast in the middle of the oven for about 10 minutes or until golden, stirring halfway through. Allow to cool.

Lightly oil the base and sides of an 11 x 17 x 2-in (28 x 43 x 5-cm) baking dish. Line the dish with foil and then oil the foil. Cover the base of the dish with one-third of the toasted coconut. Set aside the remaining coconut in an airtight container.

Combine the gelatin and ⅔ cup (150ml) of the water in the bowl of an electric mixer. Combine the sugar, syrup, remaining water and salt in a heavy saucepan. Bring to a boil and cook over high heat until a sugar thermometer inserted reads 240°F/116°C (or until a small amount dropped into cold water forms a soft ball when pressed between finger and thumb).

Using the whisk attachment of the electric mixer, whisk the hot syrup very slowly into the gelatin mixture, until the whole mixture is very stiff, about 15 minutes. Beat in the coconut extract. Pour the mixture over the foil-lined, coconut-covered baking dish. Hold the dish with two hands and tap on a countertop to level the surface. Cover with ⅓ of the toasted coconut. Cover with plastic wrap and leave to rest at room temperature for 12 hours.

Place the remaining coconut in a large mixing bowl. Turn the marshmallow out onto a clean work surface. Using a large knife (dipped in water if it gets sticky) cut the marshmallow into 2-in (5-cm) squares. Working in batches, toss the marshmallow squares in the bowl with the remaining coconut, pressing lightly to adhere.

Store in an airtight container at room temperature for 1 week.

Coconut marshmallows

Kids' cookies

Throughout this chapter you will find the results from careful cookie test runs with our discerning panel of pre-teen judges. Children make the best testers. They are honest and their palates are pure. Their comments were harsh at times, but sometimes tough love carves a pathway to success.

Our test products came from our own memories. The cookies we loved, the ones we remembered, the recipes we would equally enjoy as grown-ups. We baked, we made hypotheses, then we presented. What we didn't predict were two basic variables: there had to be color, interest and preferably a mix of both. A brown blob of what could be pure deliciousness just didn't cut it. Bring on the hundreds and thousands, the jelly fingers, the gorpies studded with sweets. Shards of coconut helped. Sweetness definitely elicited top marks. The most satisfying, then, was the batch of Soft banana-blueberry cookies (page 98). Not much sugar, but a lot of flavor. The little ones loved them. Then again, that panel was under the age of two.

Either way, we've amassed a collection that we hope children around the world will enjoy. If not, it's the panel who is to blame.

Hundreds and thousands cookies
Rainbow

These were always a favorite of mine right up until my teens. I think it's the lurid pink icing and multi-colored hundreds and thousands that really appeal to the young (or the young at heart).

Makes 20–24

1 cup (250g) **butter, softened**
¾ cup (140g) **confectioners sugar, sifted**
1 tsp **vanilla extract**
1 **egg yolk**
3¼ cups (375g) **all-purpose flour**

To decorate:
1 quantity **Colored icing using pink food coloring** (see page 164)
Hundreds and thousands

Beat the butter, icing sugar, vanilla extract and egg yolk together in a large bowl until creamy. Stir in the flour and mix to a firm dough. Wrap the dough in baking parchment and chill for about 30 minutes.

Preheat the oven to 375°F/190°C.

Line two baking sheets with baking parchment. Roll the dough out to about ¼in (5mm) thick and, using a square cutter, cut out shapes and transfer to the prepared sheets. Bake for 10–12 minutes, or until lightly golden. Transfer to a wire rack and allow to cool completely.

Ice each cookie with the pink icing and sprinkle with a generous amount of hundreds and thousands, covering the icing completely. Allow to set, then store in an airtight container.

Hundreds and thousands cookies

Jelly fingers

Jelly fingers

Simplicity

An easy way to please young partygoers. Make an array of different colors for full effect, using different gelatin flavors and food colorings.

Makes 24

2 Tbsp **raspberry gelatin crystals**
2½ cups (280g) **sweetened shredded coconut**
½ tsp **red food coloring**
24 **bought ladyfingers**

Place the gelatin crystals in a large bowl and pour over 1¼ cups (300ml) boiling water. Stir to dissolve, then cool the gelatin until it is of egg white consistency, about 20–30 minutes (keep a close eye on it as it will change quickly).

While the gelatin is cooling, place the coconut in a large plastic bag, add the food coloring and tie the bag tightly. Rub and shake the coconut in the food coloring until it turns an even pink color throughout.

One by one dip the ladyfingers into the gelatin mixture to coat completely, then roll in the colored coconut. Place on a wire rack to set and continue until all are dipped and coated. Allow then to set for at least 1 hour before serving.

■ *Try using different gelatin flavors and food colorings.*

Chocolate peppermint cookies
Minty

Eat them while they are still warm, and the oozy peppermint center will drizzle down your chin. It might be safer to serve them cold to the kids!

Makes 18–20

1½ sticks (150g) **butter, softened**
¾ cup (150g) **extra-fine sugar**
1 **egg yolk**
2¼ cups (250g) **all-purpose flour**
1 tsp **baking powder**
¼ cup (25g) **cocoa powder**
Approx 2 x 2oz (120g) **peppermint patties**
1 quantity **Colored icing using green food coloring** (see page 164)

Preheat the oven to 375°F/190°C. Line two baking sheets with baking parchment.

Beat the butter and sugar together in a large bowl until pale and creamy. Add the egg yolk and mix to combine. In a separate bowl sift the flour, baking powder and cocoa powder. Stir the dry ingredients into the butter and mix well to form a stiff dough.

Roll out about one-third of the mixture to about ⅛–⅛in (2–3mm) thick and, using a 2–2¼-in (5–5.5-cm) round cutter, cut out as many rounds as possible. Using a palette knife, transfer the rounds onto the baking sheets, leaving a little space between them to allow for spreading. Place one square of chocolate in the center of each round. Roll out the remaining dough to the same thickness and cut larger rounds using a 2¾–3-in (7–7.5-cm) round cutter. Place the larger rounds over the chocolate-topped rounds and seal well around the edges. Don't worry if the tops crack a little.

Bake the cookies for about 10 minutes, then allow to cool on the baking sheet for a further 5 minutes. Transfer to a wire rack and allow to cool completely before making the green icing.

Drizzle the icing over the cookies in a zigzag pattern and leave to set.

Chocolate peppermint cookies

Hokey pokey cookies
Toffee-flavored

Hokey pokey are crunchy pieces of toffee that are immersed in vanilla ice cream. This ice cream is a New Zealand icon that is second only to plain vanilla. These cookies have similar crunchy toffee characteristics and they are great with a large glass of milk.

Makes 20–24

1 stick (125g) **butter, softened**
¾ cup (150g) **extra-fine sugar**
1 Tbsp **milk**
1 Tbsp **corn syrup**
1 tsp **baking soda**
2 cups (225g) **all-purpose flour**

Preheat the oven to 350°F/180°C. Line a baking sheet with baking parchment.

Put the butter, sugar, milk and corn syrup in a saucepan and melt gently until almost boiling. Remove from the heat and cool for about 15–20 minutes. Combine with the baking soda and flour and stir into the butter mixture.

Roll the mixture into tablespoon-sized balls and place on the baking sheet. Press down with a fork and bake for 15–18 minutes, or until golden.

■ *Add 2 tsp ground ginger to make ginger cookies.*

Peanut brownies

Nutty

Traditionally, in my family, these have always been made with peanuts still in their skins. I know some people prefer them without, so I'll leave it up to you.

Makes 24

1 stick (125g) **butter,** softened
1 cup (200g) **extra-fine sugar**
1 **egg,** lightly beaten
2 cups (225g) **all-purpose flour**
1 tsp **baking powder**
1 pinch **salt**
3 Tbsp **cocoa powder**
2 cups (200g) **unsalted peanuts,**
    in their skins, or without (optional)

Preheat the oven to 350°F/180°C. Line a large baking sheet with baking parchment.

Cream the butter and sugar until pale. Add the egg and beat to combine. In a separate bowl combine the flour, baking powder, salt and cocoa powder and add to the creamed mixture. Combine until a stiff mixture forms, then stir in the peanuts until evenly dispersed.

Roll the mixture into heaped tablespoon-sized balls and place on the baking sheet, leaving a little space between them to allow for spreading.

Bake for 14–16 minutes, or until firm to the touch. Remove from the oven, transfer to a wire rack and allow to cool completely.

Lolly cake

Lolly cake

Sweet

It may only be New Zealanders who know what lolly cake is so here is my chance to share this childhood memory with the world.

Makes 1 log

1 stick (100g) **butter,** melted
9oz (250g) **graham crackers (or any plain sweet cracker),** crushed
scant 1 cup (200ml) **sweetened condensed milk**
1 cup (200g) **foam candy (e.g. circus peanuts)**
½ cup (30g) **sweetened shredded coconut**

Combine the melted butter, crackers, condensed milk and sweets in a large bowl and mix to combine.

On a large, flat surface lay out a piece of baking parchment about 18in (45cm) long. Put the cracker mixture onto the paper and manipulate it into a log shape about 10in (25cm) long. Roll up the paper and tighten the log so it stretches to about 12in (30cm) long. Open the paper again and sprinkle over the coconut. Roll the log in the coconut until evenly coated, then roll up tightly in the baking parchment. Tear off a large piece of foil and place the log on the foil. Roll up tightly, securing the ends, then refrigerate overnight or until firm.

Unwrap the log and slice into pieces to serve.

Peanut butter cookies

Comforting

These meltingly soft peanut butter concoctions, punctuated by crunchy nuts, will put a smile on all faces, young and old.

Makes 38–40

1 stick (110g) **butter,** softened
½ cup (100g) **extra-fine sugar**
scant ½ cup (80g) **light brown sugar**
1 **egg,** lightly beaten
1 cup (220g) **creamy peanut butter**
2½ cups (300g) **all-purpose flour**
½ tsp **salt**
1 tsp **baking soda**
scant 1 cup (80g) **chopped peanuts or walnuts,** toasted

Preheat the oven to 350°F/180°C.

In a large mixing bowl cream the butter and sugars until smooth. Beat in the egg and peanut butter and continue to beat until combined. In a separate bowl, sift the flour, salt and baking soda together. Add to the peanut butter mixture and stir just until combined. Stir in the toasted nuts.

Drop rounded teaspoonfuls of the mixture onto the baking sheet and depress the balls lightly with the prongs of a fork. Bake for 8–10 minutes, until just cooked through. Allow to cool for 5 minutes on the baking sheet, then transfer to wire racks and allow to cool completely.

■ *For added smiles, add 3½oz (100g) chopped chocolate to the cookie dough when you add the chopped nuts.*

Ranger cookies

Chewy

This favorite family recipe is as much of a hit with the grown-ups as it is with the kids. The distinctive texture comes from the cornflakes, which add crunch, the coconut, which adds texture, and the dates, which add moisture and sweetness.

Makes approx. 50

2 sticks (220g) **butter**
¾ cup (180g) **extra-fine sugar**
1½ cups (220g) **brown sugar**
2 **eggs**
3 cups (200g) **sweetened shredded coconut**
1½ cups (275g) **dates, finely chopped**
3¼ cups (375g) **all-purpose flour**
1 tsp **baking powder**
7 cups (160g) **cornflakes**

Preheat the oven to 350°F/180°C.

Cream the butter and sugars until light and fluffy. Add the eggs, one at a time, beating until smooth. Stir in the coconut and dates. Sift the flour and baking powder together and stir into batter. Work the cornflakes into the batter (it is easiest to use your hands for this) until roughly combined.

Form into rounded tablespoon-sized balls and place on ungreased baking sheets 2in (5cm) apart. Bake for 15 minutes, or until lightly golden. Allow to cool on the baking sheets for 5 minutes, then transfer to wire racks and allow to cool completely.

Gingerbread men
Easygoing

It's hard to find a recipe for gingerbread men that is both easy to roll and decorate and delicious to eat. Well, here it is, straight from the Jamieson family kitchen, where the queens of cookie decorating reside. Play with cookie cutters – this recipe isn't exclusive to men!

The yield depends on the size of cutter used. If you use 3½-in (9-cm) cutters, you will have 7 gingerbread men.

1¼ cups (150g) **butter**
¾ cup (130g) **extra-fine sugar**
1 **egg**
scant 1 cup (200ml) **molasses**
4 cups (450g) **all-purpose flour**
½ tsp **baking powder**
1 tsp **baking soda**
1 tsp **salt**
1 tsp **ground ginger**
½ tsp **ground cloves**
½ tsp **ground cinnamon**

Suggested decorations:
Royal eggnog icing (see page 164)
Silver balls
Chocolate drops
Hundreds and thousands

Combine the butter and sugar in a large bowl and beat, using an electric mixer, until light and fluffy. Add the egg and molasses and beat until smooth. In a separate bowl, sift the flour with the baking powder, soda, salt, cinnamon and cloves. Slowly add the flour mixture to the molasses mixture in three separate stages, stirring with a wooden spoon until combined.

Divide the dough into four balls, flatten and wrap in plastic wrap then refrigerate for at least 1 hour before use.

Preheat the oven to 375°F/190°C.

Roll the balls, one at a time, between two sheets of wax paper to a ⅛-in (3-mm) thickness. Peel off the top layer and cut into patterns. Carefully transfer cut-outs to ungreased baking trays. Bake for 10–15 minutes, until just cooked. Do not over-cook. Allow the gingerbread men to cool on trays, for 5 minutes, then transfer to racks and allow to cool completely. Decorate as you wish.

■ *The recipe can easily be doubled, or made in advance. Wrap dough in plastic wrap and freeze for up to 1 month. Allow to thaw in the fridge overnight before using.*

Gingerbread men

Great gorpies

Universal

"Gorp" is the great energy booster mix made of peanuts, raisins and chocolate chips. It is eaten in handfuls, and here is also added in handfuls. All right, my kids' panel has revised gorp to include simply M&M's® and peanuts. Raisins are also a welcome addition. This recipe is egg-free.

Makes 32

2 sticks (220g) **butter, softened**
1½ cups (200g) **brown sugar**
1 grown-up handful **peanuts**
    (about ½ cup/100g)
1 grown-up handful **M&M's®**
    (about ½ cup/100g)
1¼ cups (140g) **whole wheat flour**
1¼ cups (140g) **all-purpose flour**
1 tsp **baking soda**
2 tsp **milk**

Preheat the oven to 350°F/180°C. Grease or line two baking sheets with baking parchment.

Beat the butter and sugar together until smooth. Stir in the peanuts and M&M's®. Sift the flours together with the baking soda and add to the butter mixture. Add the milk and stir to combine. Shape the dough into rounded tablespoonfuls with your hands and drop the mounds onto greased or parchment-lined baking sheets.

Bake for 10–12 minutes, just until set. Allow to cool on the baking sheets for 5 minutes, then transfer to wire racks and allow to cool completely.

Oatmeal raisin cookies

Warming

Our version of this classic cookie is very chewy. It's packed with oats and raisins, and features a lovely hint of cinnamon.

Makes 35

1½ sticks (165g) **butter, softened**
1 cup (150g) **brown sugar**
generous ½ cup (110g) **extra-fine sugar**
1 **egg**
2 Tbsp **water**
2 tsp **vanilla extract**
1 cup (120g) **all-purpose flour**
⅛ tsp **salt**
1 tsp **baking soda**
1 tsp **ground cinnamon**
2¾ cups (300g) **dry quick oatmeal**
1½ cups (220g) **raisins**

Preheat the oven to 350°F/180°C.

Beat the butter and sugars in an electric mixer until light and fluffy. Beat in the egg, water and vanilla extract until combined. In a separate bowl, sift together the flour, salt, baking soda and cinnamon. Add to the butter mixture along with the oats and raisins, stirring just until combined.

Roll the dough into tablespoon-sized balls with your hands and place 2in (5cm) apart on ungreased baking sheets. Bake for 12–14 minutes, until the edges are crispy but the centers are soft and bubbling. Remove from the oven and allow to cool on the baking sheets for 5 minutes. Don't over-bake – the cookies will continue to cook on the sheets. Transfer to wire racks and allow to cool completely.

Store the cookies in an airtight container for 3–5 days, or freeze for up to 2 months.

Popcorn balls

Popcorn balls

Sticky

Thanks once again to Aunt Sandra for these delectable balls. They are chewy, not at all dry, and incredibly similar in flavor to Cracker Jacks.

Makes 10–14

3½ cups (70g) **popped popcorn**
generous 1 cup (250ml) **molasses** (see tip)
¾ cup (150g) **extra-fine sugar**
2 Tbsp **white vinegar**
2 Tbsp **butter**
½ cup (125ml) **water**
½ tsp **baking soda**
1¾ cups (200g) **pecans or walnuts,** chopped (or a combination of both)

Put the popped popcorn into two large, separate bowls (this will make combining with the molasses syrup a much easier task). Set aside.

Combine the molasses, sugar, white vinegar, butter and water in a saucepan over medium heat. Boil gently, without stirring, until the mixture begins to bubble and a sugar thermometer inserted reads 240°F/116°C (or until a small amount dropped into cold water forms a soft ball when pressed between finger and thumb). Stir in the baking soda. Working quickly, pour the syrup over the two bowls of popcorn. Add the chopped nuts and stir to combine.

When the popcorn is cool enough to handle, butter your hands, scoop up the popcorn by the fistful and roll into balls. Wrap each ball individually in plastic wrap.

Hundreds and thousands ice cream sandwiches
Colorful

Hundreds and thousands, commonly yet boringly called "sprinkles," are enough to make any child smile. Sprinkled over a cookie and sandwiched around creamy ice cream makes for sheer bliss!

Makes 10–15

1 quantity **Hundreds and thousands cookies** (see page 78)
4½ cups (1L) **strawberry (or any favorite) ice cream,** slightly softened
Extra hundreds and thousands, for decorating

Place half the cookies, hundreds and thousands-side down, on a work surface. Spoon softened strawberry ice cream about 1in (2cm) thick on the underside of each cookie. Place a matching cookie on top of the ice cream, top-side facing up. Sprinkle the exposed ice cream with more hundreds and thousands.

Place the sandwich in an airtight container and immediately transfer to the freezer to harden completely. Repeat with the remaining ice cream and cookies. Store the sandwiches in airtight container in the freezer for 3–4 days.

Hundreds and thousands ice cream sandwiches

Soft banana-blueberry cookies

Flavorsome

Mom-and-baby play dates are great for sharing recipes, and these cookies passed the toddler test with flying colors. Substitute blueberries for other berries, if you prefer, or use finely chopped raisins or cranberries.

Makes 30-32

1 **ripe medium banana,** mashed
⅓ cup (75g) **butter (see tip),** softened
generous ¼ cup (40g) **brown sugar**
¼ cup (75ml) **apple juice**
1 **egg**
½ tsp **vanilla extract**
⅔ cup (75g) **all-purpose flour**
½ tsp **baking soda**
¾ cup (50g) **dry quick oatmeal**
scant ½ cup (75g) **blueberries,** fresh
   or frozen

Preheat the oven to 350°F/180°C. Lightly grease a baking sheet or line it with baking parchment.

Combine the mashed banana, butter and brown sugar in a mixing bowl and stir until combined. Add apple juice, egg and vanilla, and stir until smooth. In a separate bowl, sift the flour with the baking soda. Add to the banana mixture along with the oats. Carefully add the blueberries – too much stirring at this point will turn the batter blue!

Drop the batter by the teaspoonful onto the prepared baking sheet, spacing the mounds about 2in (5cm) apart. Bake for 10 minutes, until set. Allow to cool on the baking sheet for 5 minutes, then transfer to wire racks and allow to cool completely. Store the cookies in an airtight container for up to 5 days, or freeze for up to 2 months.

■ *You can substitute soy or peanut butter for the butter if you prefer.*

Witchy fingers

Creepy

Thanks to Diane Nichols for sharing the recipe for these tasty, yet very eerie, Halloween fingers.

Makes approx. 26–28

2 sticks (220g) **butter**
scant 1 cup (125g) **confectioners sugar**
1 **egg**
1 tsp **almond extract**
1 tsp **vanilla extract**
3¾–4 cups (425–450g) **all-purpose flour**
1 tsp **baking powder**
1 tsp **salt**
About 30 **sliced almonds**
Red decorating gel (optional)

Preheat the oven to 350°F/180°C. Line two baking sheets with baking parchment.

Cream the butter and confectioners sugar in an electric mixer until light and fluffy. Add the egg together with the almond and vanilla extracts and beat until smooth. In a separate bowl, sift the flour with the baking powder and salt. Add to the butter mixture and stir to combine. Add a little more flour if the dough feels sticky.

Roll the dough into tablespoon-sized balls then form into index finger-shaped logs and place on baking sheets. Flatten slightly at the knuckles and make little wrinkle lines with the tip of a knife. Put a drop of red decorating gel at the tip of each finger, if using, and stick a sliced almond over to form a fingernail. Don't worry if the almonds are cracked – that only adds to the creepiness of the fingers!

Bake for 12–15 minutes, until the fingers are golden and cooked through. Allow to cool on the baking sheets, then transfer to wire racks to cool completely.

Store in airtight containers for 3–5 days, or freeze for up to 2 months.

Coffee-time cookies

Coffee. Tea. Cookies. What does this mean to you?

To my grandmother, it's a gathering of women from her church group. Grammy will serve something with ginger, something lacy, and something with a touch of jam. The ladies will carefully perch on sofas and chairs, teacups in one hand, a cookie in the other, a pretty napkin placed on their laps. Bites will be savored, but over-eating is out of the question.

To others it could be an afternoon on the beach, when the grill is dying down. People sit around the fire, drinking tea and eating freshly baked cookies from a tin. With toes nestled in the sand, they take a sip, take a bite, take another sip. One cup is never enough, nor is one cookie.

Or how about the morning-coffee party, the ones where good friends gather to lounge on overstuffed sofas. The aroma of freshly ground coffee emanates from the kitchen and stories are flowing. Chocolate is necessary here, or perhaps a touch of espresso-studded shortbread.

To everyone, however, it all boils down to a few basic needs: friendship, hot drinks and cookies.

Biscotti

Biscotti

Traditional

Biscotti is the plural of biscotto, which literally means "twice baked" in Italian. This method of baking produces a very hard, crunchy cookie, which is delicious dunked in vin santo (Tuscan dessert wine) or served with a cup of coffee.

Makes approx. 30

2¼ cups (250g) **all-purpose flour**
¾ cup (150g) **extra-fine sugar**
1 tsp **baking powder**
generous ½ cup (100g) **crystalized ginger,** cut into chunks
1¼ cups (125g) **Brazil nuts,** chopped into chunks
3 **eggs**

Variation:
Omit the crystalized ginger and Brazil nuts and add:
1½ cups (200g) **whole almonds,** blanched
5½oz (150g) **bittersweet chocolate,** cut into chunks
Or:
1½ cups (150g) **pistachio nuts**
5½oz (150g) **bittersweet chocolate,** cut into chunks

Preheat the oven to 350°F/180°C. Line two large baking sheets with baking parchment and set aside.

Put all the dry ingredients in a large bowl and mix to combine. Add the eggs and stir until the mixture comes together in a ball, adding a little extra flour if it is too wet. Halve the mixture and place each half on the baking parchment. Shape into long, flat log shapes about 10in (25cm) long, 4in (10cm) wide and 1in (2.5cm) high. Bake for about 20 minutes, or until the logs are cooked through and only very lightly golden.

Remove from the oven and, when they are cool enough to handle, lift the logs onto a board, and slice thinly (about ⅜in/7mm thick) on the diagonal, then place the separate cookies back flat on the baking sheets. Bake for 10 minutes, then turn and bake for a further 5 minutes on the other side or until lightly golden and crispy. Transfer to a wire rack and allow to cool completely.

These will keep in an airtight container for about 7–10 days.

Berry chocolate florentines

Decadent

These large flat cookies are usually made with candied peel and glacé cherries instead of the mixed dried berries. Chocolate-dipped or not, they are simply divine!

Makes 12

⅓ cup (75g) **butter**
½ cup (75g) **light brown sugar**
½ cup (50g) **all-purpose flour**
½ cup (50g) **sliced almonds,** toasted
scant ½ cup (100g) **mixed dried berries, e.g. cranberries, blueberries, cherries, strawberries**
5½oz (150g) **unsweetened baking chocolate,** chopped
¼–½ tsp **pumpkin-pie spice**

Preheat the oven to 350°F/180°C. Line a large baking sheet with baking parchment.

Heat the butter and sugar together in a saucepan until the sugar dissolves and they bind together. Remove from the heat and mix in the flour, then add the nuts and berries.

Put tablespoonfuls of the mixture, quite widely spaced, on the baking sheet and flatten slightly using the back of the spoon. You may need to bake them in two batches.

Bake the florentines for 10–12 minutes, or until spread flat and golden. While still hot, neaten up the edges using a knife and allow to cool completely on the baking sheet. Melt the chocolate over a saucepan of simmering water or in the microwave. Stir in the pumpkin-pie spice and mix well. Using a palette knife, spread the chocolate over the flat side of the florentines and allow to cool before serving.

Berry chocolate florentines

Ricciarelli

Delicate

These little diamond-shaped cookies make the perfect gift.

Makes 24

1½ cups (200g) **ground almonds**
1½ cups (200g) **confectioners sugar**, sifted
1 Tbsp **all-purpose flour**
½ tsp **baking powder**
2 **egg whites**
1 tsp **amaretto or rum**
Grated rind of 1 **orange**
scant ½ cups (50g) **confectioners sugar**, sifted, for rolling

Preheat the oven to 275°F/140°C. Line two baking sheets with baking parchment.

Combine the ground almonds, sifted confectioners sugar, flour and baking powder in a large bowl. Mix well to combine. In a separate bowl beat the egg whites until stiff peaks form. Mix the egg whites into the almond mixture, along with the amaretto and orange rind.

Place the extra confectioners sugar in a separate shallow bowl. Form the mixture into heaped teaspoon-sized balls and roll them in the extra confectioners sugar. Form each ball into a diamond shape, using the palm of your hand to flatten them and your fingers to pinch in the sides.

Bake for 25–30 minutes, or until firm and lightly golden.

Gingernuts
Crunchy

These are the perfect balance between crunchy and chewy. I put them to the test on Lottie Davies and Tom Norrington-Davies, photographer and food writer respectively. They passed with flying colors, as a further four were consumed over breakfast. What more can I say!

Makes 16

½ stick (60g) **butter**
1 Tbsp **candied gingerroot syrup**
scant ½ cup (100ml) **corn syrup**
1 tsp **baking soda**
1 Tbsp **preserved gingerroot (about 2 pieces)**, finely chopped
1⅔ cups (200g) **all-purpose flour**
¾ cup (100g) **light brown sugar**

Preheat the oven to 325°F/160°C. Line two baking sheets with baking parchment.

Place the butter, gingerroot syrup and corn syrup in a saucepan and stir over low heat until the butter has melted. Add the baking soda and allow it to foam. Remove from the heat, stir in the gingerroot and set aside.

Put the flour and sugar in a large mixing bowl and mix to combine. Add the butter mixture and stir well. Roll heaped tablespoons of the mixture into balls and place them on the baking sheet, leaving enough space to allow for spreading.

Bake for 18–20 minutes, or until firm. Leave on the baking sheet for a few minutes, then transfer to a wire rack and allow to cool completely.

Ginger kisses

Ginger kisses

Melt-in-your-mouth

Filled with a delicately sweet ginger cream, these are definitely the ones to impress the in-laws with!

Makes 20–24

1 cup (250g) **butter, softened**
scant 1 cup (115g) **confectioners sugar**, sifted
1 **egg,** lightly beaten
3 tsp **ground ginger**
2 cups (225g) **all-purpose flour**
1 cup (150g) **cornstarch**

For the filling:
generous 1 cup (250g) **mascarpone**
1 Tbsp (50g) **candied gingerroot,** finely chopped
1 Tbsp **gingerroot syrup**
¼ cup (50g) **demerara sugar** (see page 12)
½ tsp **vanilla extract**

Preheat the oven to 325°F/170°C. Line two baking sheets with baking parchment.

In a large bowl beat the butter until pale and creamy. Gradually add the confectioners sugar, beating well after each addition until the mixture is light and fluffy. Beat in the egg until well combined. If the mixture starts to curdle, add a tablespoon of the flour. In a separate bowl combine the ginger, flour and cornstarch. Sift the dry ingredients into the butter mixture and mix thoroughly. Roll teaspoon-sized amounts into balls and press down with a fork.

Bake for 20–22 minutes, or until firm and lightly golden in color. Transfer to a wire rack and allow to cool completely.

While the cookies are cooling, prepare the filling. Combine all the ingredients in a bowl and set aside. When the cookies are cool enough, spread the filling on half the cookies, then place the remaining cookies on top.

■ *If the mixture is too firm to pipe, stand it in warm water for a few minutes.*

Bumblebees

Nostalgic

Bumblebees are a real childhood memory. Mum used to make them for every school gala or fair. They last for ages and are also a great Christmas time standby.

Makes 30–36

generous ½ cup (150g) **dates**
scant 1 cup (150g) **golden raisins**
¾ cup (125g) **walnuts**
1 Tbsp (50g) **candied gingerroot,** roughly chopped
¾ cup (100g) **dried figs (about** 6–8**)**
1½ cups (375ml) **sweetened condensed milk**
1½ cups (100g) **sweetened shredded coconut,** plus extra for coating

Preheat the oven to 325°F/160°C. Line a large baking sheet with baking parchment.

Put the dates, raisins, walnuts, gingerroot and figs in a food processor and pulse to a coarse mince. Transfer the mixture to a large bowl and add the condensed milk and coconut. Stir well to combine. Roll the mixture into tablespoon-sized balls and coat in extra coconut, then place on the lined baking sheet. Repeat until all the mixture is used up.

Bake for 25–30 minutes, or until lightly golden.

These can be stored in an airtight container for up to 1 month.

Espresso shortbread slice

Sophisticated

Whether cut into thin or thick slices, these delicious shortbreads are bound to perk up any coffee moment.

Makes 6 x 4-in (10-cm) tartlets
    or 2 x 8-in (20-cm) tarts

2 sticks (220g) **butter**
1½ cups (200g) **extra-fine sugar**
1 **egg yolk**
2 tsp **vanilla extract**
2½ cups (300g) **all-purpose flour**
1½ tsp **baking powder**
2 Tbsp **espresso coffee beans,**
    finely ground

For the topping:
5½oz (150g) **unsweetened baking**
    chocolate
1 Tbsp **cold coffee**
1 Tbsp **butter**

Preheat the oven to 350°F/180°C. Lightly grease six 4-in (10-cm) tartlet pans or two 8-in (20-cm) flan pans.

Using an electric mixer, beat the butter and sugar until light and fluffy. Add the egg yolk and vanilla extract and beat until combined. In a separate bowl sift together the flour and baking powder.

Stir in the ground espresso beans. Add the flour mixture to the butter mixture and stir briefly, then tip the mixture onto a lightly floured board and knead together with your hands until combined.

Divide the dough into six (or two) equal parts and pat the dough into your chosen tart pans. Bake for 20 minutes, until golden. Transfer the pans to wire racks and allow to cool completely.

While the shortbread is cooling, make the topping. Melt the chocolate in a double boiler. As it melts, add the coffee and butter and stir to combine. If the chocolate is quite thick once melted, add a little more coffee. Using the prongs of a fork, drizzle the melted chocolate over the shortbread. (Flick with your wrist – making a bit of a mess is mandatory!).

Allow to cool completely before removing the shortbread from the pans. Slice and serve. Store the remaining shortbread in an airtight container for up to 3 days.

Raspberry Shrewsburys

Irresistibly sweet

I had always known of these cookies as Raspberry Shrewsburys until I came to England. After making them at the photo shoot and hearing everyone call them Jammy dodgers, I simply had to convert. Buttery cookies sandwiched together with raspberry jam, these are good at coffee time and also make a lunch box treat.

Makes 20

2¼ cups (250g) **flour**
1½ sticks (175g) **butter**
¾ cup (125g) **extra-fine sugar**
1 large **egg yolk**
scant 1 cup (200g) **raspberry jam**
Juice of 1 **lemon**

Put the flour and butter in a food processor and process until the mixture resembles breadcrumbs. Add the sugar and egg yolk and process until the mixture starts to form a dough. Alternatively, cut the butter into small cubes and add to the flour. Using your fingers, rub the butter into the flour until it makes fine breadcrumbs. Add the sugar and egg yolks and mix to a smooth dough.

On a lightly floured surface knead the dough until it comes together. Shape into a ball and wrap in baking parchment and chill for at least 30 minutes.

Preheat the oven to 325°F/170°C. Line a baking sheet with baking parchment.

Roll out the dough on a lightly floured surface to about ⅛in (3mm) thick and cut out rounds using a 2–2½-in (5–6-cm) crimped cutter. Re-roll the trimmings and cut out more rounds until you have 40. Use a ½-in (1-cm) piping tip to remove the center from 20 of the rounds.

Bake for 10–12 minutes, or until lightly golden in color. Remove from the oven and allow to cool for a few minutes on the baking sheet, then transfer to a wire rack and allow to cool completely.

While the cookies are cooling, put the jam and lemon juice in a saucepan and heat to a simmer. Spoon or brush the jam over the base of a whole round and sandwich with a round with its center removed on top. Continue until all are done. Allow to cool completely.

Raspberry Shrewsburys

Classic shortbread

Classic shortbread

Angelic

This recipe comes from Elizabeth Green, who used to run a café and bakery in Halifax, Nova Scotia. The recipe is from her Great Aunt Josie, who came from Prince Edward Island. It is the best shortbread I've ever tasted and, in the words of my brother-in-law, they taste as if they've been "kissed by an angel."

Makes 40 x 2-in (5-cm) diameter cookies

scant ½ cup (50g) **confectioners sugar,** sifted
2 cups (450g) **butter,** softened
1 tsp **vanilla extract**
½ cup (60g) **cornstarch,** sifted
4⅔ cups (525g) **all-purpose flour,** sifted

Preheat the oven to 350°F/180°C.

Combine the sifted confectioners sugar and butter in a large mixing bowl and beat until very light and fluffy. Add the vanilla extract and beat until smooth. In a separate bowl, combine the sifted flour and cornstarch. Using a wooden spoon, stir the flour mixture into the butter mixture and work together until combined.

Divide the dough into two equal mounds. Flour a work surface and roll the first mound into a 9½-in (24-cm) wide circle, almost ⅝in (1.5cm) thick. Cut the dough into desired shapes and place on parchment-lined baking sheets. (We used a 2-in [5-cm] wide round wooden thistle mold, but you can use an ordinary round cutter.)

Bake for 15–20 minutes, until slightly golden. Allow to cool for 5 minutes, then transfer to wire racks and allow to cool completely.

Meanwhile, continue baking the remaining shortbread. Top the shortbread, if liked, with a swirl of Vanilla butter icing (see page 166).

Almond and quince thumbprints

Comforting

Thumbprints are a comforting, jam-centered, old-fashioned cookie. Here they take on a slightly modern twist with the addition of quince jelly. However, any jelly or jam will do.

Makes 30

½ cup (110g) **extra-fine sugar**
2 sticks (220g) **butter, softened**
½ cup (60g) **confectioners sugar**
1¼ cups (150g) **whole almonds,**
    blanched, toasted and ground
    to a fine powder
1 **egg yolk**
1 tsp **vanilla extract**
½ tsp **almond essence**
2½ cups (300g) **all-purpose flour**
½ tsp **baking powder**
¼ tsp **salt**
½ cup (125g) **quince jelly**

Preheat the oven to 350°F/180°C.

Using an electric mixer, beat the sugar and butter until light and fluffy. Beat in the confectioners sugar, ground almonds, egg yolk, vanilla extract and almond essence. In a separate bowl, sift together the flour, baking powder and salt. Add to the butter mixture and stir just until combined.

Shape rounded teaspoonfuls of the dough into balls and place on ungreased baking sheets about 2in (5cm) apart. Make an indentation in the center of each ball with your thumb, or with the end of a wooden spoon. Fill the indentations with ¼ tsp quince jelly. Bake for 12 minutes, or until the cookies are golden. Cool on the baking sheets for 5 minutes, then transfer to wire racks and allow to cool completely.

Almond and quince thumbprints

Panforte

Panforte (Pan-for-tā´)

Reminiscent

Panforte, a specialty from the Italian city of Siena, means "strong bread." We prefer to think of it as "beautiful, edible, sweet stained glass," but that's too wordy. Our version features very untraditional pistachio nuts, apricots and ground cardamom for a touch of Middle Eastern flair.

Makes 1 x 9-in (23-cm) cake

scant 1 cup (100g) **shelled pistachio nuts**
¾ cup (100g) **almonds**
1 cup (100g) **dried apricots,** roughly chopped
¾ cup (100g) **candied peel,** roughly chopped
¾ cup (50g) **sweetened shredded coconut**
Grated rind of 1 **lemon**
1 tsp **ground cardamom**
½ cup (75g) **all-purpose flour**
¾ cup (150g) **extra-fine sugar**
4 Tbsp **honey**
½ stick (50g) **butter**
Confectioners sugar, for dusting

Preheat the oven to 300°F/150°C.

Line a 9-in (23-cm) spring-release pan with baking parchment or rice paper. Toast the nuts in a frying pan over medium heat, stirring occasionally until golden. Allow to cool. Place the toasted nuts in a large bowl and toss with the apricots, candied peel, coconut, lemon rind, cardamom and flour.

Combine the sugar, honey and butter in a saucepan over medium heat. Cook, stirring occasionally, until the mixture begins to bubble and a sugar thermometer inserted reads 240°F/116°C (or until a small amount dropped into cold water forms a soft ball when pressed between finger and thumb).

Pour the syrup into the nut mixture and quickly combine – it will stiffen quickly. If cool enough, use your hands to blend. Pat the mixture into the pan, press down the surface evenly and bake for 35 minutes. It will not change visually during cooking, but don't worry!

Allow to cool for 30 minutes, then run a knife around the edge. Remove the paper from beneath the *panforte*, then leave to cool completely. Dust heavily with confectioners sugar. Store in an airtight container, or thinly slice and serve.

Dessert-time cookies

I've done drastic things to satisfy my cookie cravings. I've faced the kind of adversity that would force the average person to throw in the kitchen towel. But once a craving strikes, nothing has ever stood in my way. I have found myself in ill-equipped kitchens baking cookies in a roasting pan, in microwave ovens and in a frying pan over an open fire. I've even made little cookies in the bottoms of muffin pans.

But I've learned my lesson. I now travel with my beloved baking sheet and plenty of baking parchment in my overnight bag so I can make cookies with ease and grace whenever I want.

Many cookies don't require a sophisticated kit. But there are some – the dainty, dessert-worthy kind – that are more likely to maintain their delicate status when made with the right equipment. Persian lace cookies (page 132) slip from the pan. *Langues de chat* (page 123) emerge evenly golden. Bark (page 137) bubbles uniformly under the heat.

Experience proves that any cookie is welcome for dessert, and this selection will provide all you need to round off a meal in style. People might raise an eyebrow, until, that is, they sample your cookies.

Langues de chat

Langues de chat (long da sha)

Delicate

Langues de chat means "cats' tongues" in French, and these are very appropriately named. Thin, tongue-shaped cookies that can be pepped up with a few additional flavorings if liked.

Makes approx. 36–48

1 stick (125g) **butter,** softened
scant ¾ cup (125g) **extra-fine sugar**
3 **egg whites**
1 cup (125g) **all-purpose flour**

Optional extras (choose only one from the following):
2 tsp **lavender flowers / dried rose petals / fennel seeds** or **crystalized fruits,** finely chopped
½ tsp **ground cinnamon**
½ tsp **vanilla extract**
Grated rind of 1 **orange or lemon**

Preheat the oven to 400°F/200°C. Line a baking sheet with baking parchment.

Beat the butter and sugar together until pale and creamy. In a separate bowl whisk the egg whites until stiff, then gradually fold them into the butter mixture. Sift in the flour and gently fold into the mixture.

Fit a piping bag with a medium-sized plain tip and spoon in the mixture. Pipe the mixture into 3-in (7.5-cm) long fingers, no thicker than ½in (1cm) wide, leaving a little space between them to allow for spreading.

Sprinkle with the optional extras of your choice, if liked, and bake for 5–8 minutes, or until crispy and pale golden around the edges. Allow to cool completely.

Mini macaroons

Coconutty

Macaroons are simplicity at its best. Only four ingredients are required, yet they produce an impressive result.

Makes 24–36

2¼ cups (175g) **sweetened shredded coconut**
¾ cup (150g) **extra-fine sugar**
2 **egg whites,** lightly beaten
4 sheets **edible rice paper**

Preheat the oven to 325°F/170°C.

In a large bowl combine the coconut and extra-fine sugar. Add the egg whites and stir in to form a fairly firm mixture.

Lay out the rice paper on one or two baking sheets. Shape the mixture into heaped teaspoon-sized balls and place on the rice paper, pressing down gently to flatten.

Bake for 10–12 minutes, or until lightly golden. Remove from the oven and allow to cool on the baking sheets. Tear away any excess rice paper to serve.

■ *Try adding some grated lime rind or finely shredded kaffir lime leaves to the mixture for a more exotic macaroon.*

Mini macaroons

Spiced cigar cookies

Impressive

These cookies are very delicate and require quick hands. You must work fast to achieve a neat-looking cylindrical shape, but they are well worth the effort and patience!

Makes 24–30

2 **egg whites**
½ cup (90g) **extra-fine sugar**
½ cup (50g) **all-purpose flour**
½–1 tsp **ground cinnamon,
   pumpkin-pie spice or ginger (or
   any other spice of choice)**
4 Tbsp **butter,** melted

Beat the egg whites in a large clean bowl until soft peaks form. Gradually beat in the sugar until the mixture becomes thick and glossy. In a separate bowl combine the flour and spice. Add the flour mixture and the melted butter to the egg white mixture and mix until just combined. Allow the mixture to rest for about 15 minutes.

Preheat the oven to 350°F/180°C. Line a baking sheet with baking parchment.

Spoon teaspoonfuls of the mixture onto the baking parchment and, using the back of a spoon, spread evenly and thinly to about 3¼in (8cm) in diameter. Make sure the mixture is evenly spread to ease the next stage. Bake only three or four per tray. Bake for 3 minutes, or until lightly golden.

Remove from the oven and wait for 30 seconds before loosening the cookies using a flat palette knife. Return to the oven for a further 15–20 seconds to soften the cookies again.

Remove from the oven and, working quickly, turn the cookies over and roll up thinly around a lightly greased wooden spoon handle to obtain a cylinder shape. Slide off and set aside. Repeat until all the mixture is used up.

Almond and vanilla triangles

Crisp

These are a great accompaniment to ice cream. Shaped like a triangle, they act as a perfect scoop.

Makes 16–20

1 Tbsp **all-purpose flour,** sifted
1 Tbsp **ground almonds**
¼ cup (45g) **extra-fine sugar**
1 **egg white,** lightly beaten
½ tsp **vanilla extract**
2 Tbsp **melted butter**
⅓ cup (30g) **sliced almonds**

Preheat the oven to 350°F/180°C. Line the base of a 12 x 10-in (30 x 25-cm) baking tray with baking parchment.

Combine the flour, almonds and sugar in a small bowl. Stir in the egg white, vanilla extract and melted butter and mix to a smooth batter. Pour the mixture into the prepared tray and spread evenly over the surface. Sprinkle over the sliced almonds.

Bake for 12–14 minutes, or until firm when gently pressed and lightly golden in color. Remove from the oven and transfer the baking parchment to a cutting board.

Trim the edges, working as quickly as possible, then cut the rectangle in half lengthways. Cut each half into about 8–10 triangles and transfer to a wire rack. Allow to cool completely before serving.

Sugar butter cookies

Colorful

These dessert-time cookies will really appeal to the kids if you cut them into different shapes and top each with different colored sugars.

Makes approx. 24–30

2½ cups (275g) **all-purpose flour**
2 sticks (200g) **firm butter**
¾ cup (100g) **confectioners sugar**
2 **egg yolks**
1 quantity **Clear sugar glaze**
   (see page 170)
Colored sugars (see page 167)

Put the flour and butter in a food processor and process until the mixture resembles fine breadcrumbs. Add the sugar and egg yolks and process until the mixture starts to form a dough. Alternatively, cut the butter into small cubes and add to the flour. Using your fingers, rub the butter into the flour until it makes fine breadcrumbs. Add the sugar and egg yolks and mix to a smooth dough. On a lightly floured surface knead the dough until it comes together. Shape into a ball and wrap in baking parchment, then chill for at least 30 minutes.

Preheat the oven to 375°F/190°C. Line a baking sheet with baking parchment. Roll out the dough on a lightly floured surface to about ¼in (5mm) thick and cut into your chosen shapes. Bake for 8–10 minutes, or until lightly golden in color. Remove from the oven and allow to cool for a few minutes on the baking sheet, then transfer to a wire rack and allow to cool completely.

While the cookies are still warm, brush them with the sugar glaze, then sprinkle over the colored sugar of your choice. Leave to cool completely so the sugar glaze sets.

Chocolate peanut *tuiles* (tweel)

Chocolate lace

Tuiles, meaning "tile" in French, are named after the tiled roofs of Provence. Here *tuiles* are made up of two classic ingredients to make one, lacy delight. Serve them plain, or with vanilla ice cream and a drizzle of chocolate sauce.

Makes 44–48

5 Tbsp **salted butter**
½ cup (100g) **extra-fine sugar**
3 Tbsp **corn syrup**
1 Tbsp **heavy cream**
⅓ cup (35g) **all-purpose flour**
¼ cup (40g) **cocoa powder**
¼ tsp **salt**
1 cup (100g) **salted peanuts, chopped**

Preheat the oven to 350°F/180°C. Line baking sheets with baking parchment. For rounded *tuiles*, have a rolling pin at hand.

Combine the butter, sugar, corn syrup and cream in a heavy saucepan and bring to a boil over medium heat, stirring constantly. Add the flour, cocoa powder and salt, and continue stirring until the batter is thick. Stir in the peanuts.

Drop level teaspoonfuls of the batter (level off each teaspoon with a knife) onto the baking sheet, approximately six mounds to a sheet (see tip). Bake until flat, lacy and bubbling, about 5–7 minutes. Allow to cool for 2 minutes, then quickly flip the *tuiles* over.

Leave to cool if you want flat *tuiles*. For rounded *tuiles*, quickly place 2–3 *tuiles* around a rolling pin to shape, then slide them onto a wire rack and allow to cool. If the *tuiles* become too stiff to shape, return them briefly to the oven. Continue with the remaining batter.

Store the *tuiles* in an airtight container for up to 1 week.

■ *Cook the* tuiles *six at a time. Any more, and working quickly becomes too difficult.*

Pink peppercorn meringues

Pink peppercorn meringues

Lush

Piquancy meets sweet innocence in these little cloud-like meringues. The combination may seem odd, but the hint of heat is a surprisingly welcome contrast to the delicate sweetness of meringues.

Makes 60–70

6 **egg whites**
⅛ tsp **cream of tartar**
2¼ cups (420g) **extra-fine sugar**
1 Tbsp **balsamic vinegar**
1½ tsp **pink peppercorns,** coarsely ground
Confectioners sugar, for dusting (optional)

Preheat the oven to 275°F/140°C. Line a baking sheet with baking parchment.

Place the egg whites into the bowl of an electric mixer. The bowl should be very clean. Beat the egg whites until foamy. Add the cream of tartar and continue to beat until soft peaks form. Beat the sugar in gradually, one spoonful at a time, until the whites are glossy. This will take about 10 minutes. (It may seem daunting, but stick with it!) Gently stir in the vinegar and half the peppercorns.

Spoon mounded tablespoonfuls of the meringue mixture onto the baking sheet. Sprinkle with the remaining peppercorns. Bake for 40–45 minutes, until the whites are set and are just beginning to turn golden. Remove from the oven and allow to cool. If not serving immediately, store the meringues in an airtight container for up to 1 week.

Persian lace cookies

Rose-scented

These crisp, lacy cookies, studded with vibrant pistachio nuts and a touch of rosewater, are bursting with Persian flavors.

Makes approx. 30

1¼ cups (140g) **all-purpose flour**
¼ tsp **salt**
1 cup (150g) **light brown sugar**
½ cup (125ml) **corn syrup**
1 stick (120g) **butter**
scant 1 cup (100g) **pistachio nuts, chopped**
1 Tbsp **rosewater**

Preheat the oven to 375°F/190°C. Lightly grease or line two baking sheets with parchment paper.

Sift the flour with the salt in a bowl and set aside. Combine the brown sugar, corn syrup and butter in a saucepan over medium heat. Bring to a boil, stirring occasionally. Boil for 30 seconds. Remove from the heat and stir into the flour mixture together with the chopped pistachio nuts and rosewater.

Drop the batter by the rounded tablespoonfuls, 2in (5cm) apart, onto the baking sheets. Bake for 7–10 minutes, until the edges are lightly browned. Allow to cool on the baking sheets.

Carefully remove cookies from the baking sheets and store in an airtight container for up to 5 days.

Persian lace cookies

Crystalized ginger lace cookies

Spiced

Slivers of almonds and sweet ginger flow through these crisp, lacy cookies.

Makes approx. 48

1¼ cup (140g) **all-purpose flour**
¼ tsp **salt**
½ tsp **ground ginger**
1 cup (150g) **light brown sugar**
½ cup (125ml) **corn syrup**
8 Tbsp **butter**
1 cup (110g) **almonds,** chopped
1 Tbsp **crystalized ginger,** chopped

Preheat the oven to 350°F/180°C. Lightly grease or line two baking sheets with baking parchment.

Sift the flour together with the salt and ground ginger in a bowl. Set aside.

Combine the brown sugar, corn syrup and butter in a saucepan over medium heat. Bring to a boil, stirring occasionally. Remove from the heat and add the chopped almonds and crystalized ginger. Stir into the flour mixture.

Drop the batter by the rounded ½ teaspoonful, 2in (5cm) apart, onto the baking sheets. Bake for 9–10 minutes, until the edges are lightly browned. Allow to cool on the baking sheets.

Carefully remove cookies from baking sheets and store in an airtight container for up to 5 days.

Five-spice sponge fingers

Classic

Génoise, a whole egg sponge cake, is the basis for sponge fingers. The addition of a little more flour and the Chinese five-spice mixture gives these fingers shape and a unique flavor. For classic sponge fingers, omit the five-spice powder and substitute vanilla for the orange extract.

Makes approx. 72

3 Tbsp **butter,** melted
1½ cups (175g) **all-purpose flour,** sifted
⅛ tsp **salt**
½ tsp **Chinese five-spice powder**
2 **eggs**
4 **egg yolks**
½ cup (70g) **extra-fine sugar**
1 tsp **orange extract**
Confectioners sugar, for dusting

Preheat the oven to 400°F/200°C. Line two baking sheets with baking parchment. Have a piping bag fitted with a ⅝-in (1.5-cm) plain tip ready and waiting.

Pour the melted butter into a large mixing bowl. Set aside. Combine the flour, salt and five-spice powder together and set aside.

Combine the eggs, yolks and 1 Tbsp sugar in the bowl of an electric mixer and use the whisk attachment to combine. Add the remaining sugar and whisk by hand until smooth. Re-attach the whisk attachment and whip the mixture on medium speed until soft, pale and tripled in volume, about 4–5 minutes. Whisk in the orange extract and beat for a few seconds longer. Lift the whisk from the batter – a ribbon trail should form on the surface and should hold its place for 10 seconds. If it sinks to the bottom, continue beating.

Sprinkle the egg mixture with one-third of the flour mixture. Using a rubber spatula, gently fold together just until the flour disappears. Continue adding the flour by one-thirds until just combined. Be gentle.

Slowly add this batter, a spoonful at a time, into the bowl with the melted butter. Fold together as you go with a rubber spatula. Scoop the batter into the piping bag and pipe sponge fingers ⅝in (1.5cm) wide, 3¼in (8cm) long and ⅝in (1.5cm) apart. Using a sifter, dust the sponge fingers generously with confectioners sugar. Bake for 5–6 minutes, until firm but spongy, and not yet golden. Carefully transfer the sponge fingers, with the baking parchment still attached, to a wire rack and allow to cool completely. Separate any attached fingers gently with a knife.

Bark

Bark

Addictive

Aunt Jude is to thank for this Wilson family gathering staple. She calls it "barque," which adds quite a sophisticated edge to this delicacy. And people will think it is a delicacy – you don't have to tell them what the secret ingredient is!

Makes approx. 42 pieces

2 sticks (220g) **butter**
¾ cup (120g) **brown sugar**
6oz (180g) **snack crackers**
scant 1 cup (200g) **bitterweet chocolate chips or bittersweet chocolate,** roughly chopped
scant 1 cup (100g) **sliced almonds,** lightly toasted

Preheat the oven to 400°F/200°C.

Line a baking tray with foil, shiny-side up. Cover the foil with the crackers. Do not overlap.

Melt the butter and sugar in a saucepan over medium heat. Bring the mixture to a boil, stirring well to ensure the butter and sugar are well blended. Pour the mixture over the crackers and bake for 2–4 minutes, until the butter mixture begins to bubble. Watch carefully. Remove from the oven and sprinkle with chocolate. Bake for a further 1 minute, until the chocolate is soft. Remove from the oven and spread the chocolate evenly to form an icing layer. Sprinkle with almonds. Place the tray in the fridge for about 1 hour, until cool. Remove the bark from the foil and break roughly into 2-in (5-cm) square pieces.

Store the bark in an airtight container for up to 5 days, or freeze for up to 2 months.

Celebration cookies

Food has a powerful way of triggering our senses and transporting us to past events and celebrations. Cookies, despite their diminutive size, are especially effective transporters. Celebration cookies encourage creativity. Dainty touches are expected. Festive flavors are called for, and special ingredients are provided. Batters are stirred, shaped and baked. And suddenly, with a simple waft through the kitchen, we are taken back to last year's celebration.

Bakers around the world have a collection of celebration cookies. They are passed down through the generations, connecting us through our senses to events of the past. The ritual of baking celebration cookies acts to enforce not only the significance of the recipe, but also the event itself. Anzac cookies (page 144) remind Australians and New Zealanders of their militaristic past. Orange and rum shortbread (page 154) transports many straight to Christmas. Rugelach (page 163) signifies a Jewish celebration. Valentine stained glass cookies (page 159) remind us of loved ones on Valentine's Day. And, as we bake these recipes, we are creating future memories for those around us.

Who could have guessed that baking a cookie could hold such significance?

Polenta Christmas cookies with orange icing

Fragrant

Polenta gives these cookies a slightly crunchy texture. Attach ribbons to each cookie and decorate the tree with an assortment of Christmas shapes.

Makes approx. 40

1 cup (250g) **butter,** softened
scant 1 cup (125g) **confectioners sugar**
1 **egg yolk**
Grated **rind of** 1 **orange**
2½ cups (300g) **all-purpose flour**
½ cup (75g) **polenta or fine cornmeal**
2 Tbsp **cornstarch**
1 tsp **cardamom seeds,** crushed

To decorate:
1 quantity **Orange icing (see variation to Lemon icing, page 165)**
Silver balls
Ribbon or string (if making Christmas tree decorations)

Beat the butter and sugar in a large bowl until pale and creamy. Add the egg yolk and orange rind and beat until just combined. In a separate bowl combine the remaining ingredients and stir into the butter mixture. Stir the mixture until it all comes together and forms a ball. Wrap the ball in baking parchment and chill for 20–30 minutes.

Preheat the oven to 375°F/190°C. Roll the mixture out on a floured surface to about ⅜in (7mm) thick.

Using a cutter of your choice, cut out as many shapes as possible from the rolled mixture and place on a baking sheet lined with baking parchment. Re-shape the remaining dough and roll again until all the mixture is used up. If you want to use the cookies as Christmas tree decorations, make a small hole with a skewer for the ribbon or string at the top of the shape.

Bake for 10–12 minutes, or until golden and firm. Allow to cool on a wire rack. When the cookies have cooled completely, prepare the icing. Spread the icing over the cookies, allow to set, then decorate as liked with silver balls.

Polenta Christmas cookies with orange icing

Spiced Easter cookies

Spiced Easter cookies

Crisp

These cookies make a welcome change from chocolate Easter eggs. Decorate them with colored icings and they will appeal to both young and old.

Makes 36–48, depending on
 shapes chosen

1 stick (100g) **butter, softened**
1 cup (200g) **extra-fine sugar**
1 **egg,** beaten
2½ cups (300g) **all-purpose flour**
1 tsp **baking powder**
2 tsp **pumpkin-pie spice or ground
 cinnamon**

To decorate:
1 quantity **Colored icing (see page
 164)**

In a large bowl beat the butter and extra-fine sugar together until pale and creamy. Add the egg and beat until the mixture is light and fluffy. In a separate bowl combine the flour, baking powder and pumpkin-pie spice. Add to the butter mixture and mix thoroughly. Add 1 tsp cold water to bring the dough together if you need to. Wrap the mixture in baking parchment and chill for at least 30 minutes.

Preheat the oven to 350°F/180°C. Line two baking sheets with baking parchment.

On a lightly floured surface, roll out the dough to about ¼in (4mm) thick and, using cookie cutters, stamp out shapes. Using a palette knife, lift the shapes carefully onto the baking parchment.

Bake for 15–18 minutes, or until lightly golden in color. Allow to cool on a wire rack, then ice as liked.

Anzac cookies

Nourishing

Anzac cookies touch the hearts of all New Zealanders and Australians. Based on an old recipe for Scottish oatcakes, they were made by soldiers' wives and children and sent to the men during the First World War in order to keep them well nourished. They were so good that even today they are top of the hit list!

Makes 20

1½ cups (150g) **all-purpose flour**
1½ cups (100g) **sweetened shredded coconut**
¾ cup (100g) **light brown sugar**
1 cup (100g) **dry quick oatmeal**
1 stick (125g) **butter**
1 Tbsp **corn syrup**
½ tsp **baking soda**
2 Tbsp **boiling water**

Preheat the oven to 325°F/160°C. Line a large baking sheet with baking parchment.

Place the flour, coconut, sugar and oats in a large bowl and mix well. Place the butter and corn syrup in a saucepan over medium heat and melt. Put the baking soda in a small bowl and pour over the boiling water, stirring to combine. Add the baking soda mixture to the saucepan and stir. Pour this mixture over the dry mixture and stir all the ingredients together.

Roll teaspoonfuls of the mixture into balls and place on the lined baking sheet, leaving a little space between them to allow for spreading. Flatten each ball gently with a fork.

Bake for 15–20 minutes, or until golden brown. Allow to cool slightly on the baking sheet before transferring to a wire rack.

Anzac cookies

Fortune cookies

Impressive

This is a fun way to liven up a dinner party. Be imaginative with your fortunes and you'll be guaranteed some laughs. Make them a few days in advance and store them in an airtight container.

Makes 18

2 **egg whites**
½ cup (90g) **extra-fine sugar**
½ cup (50g) **all-purpose flour**
4 Tbsp **butter,** melted

Beat the egg whites in a large clean bowl until soft peaks form. Gradually beat in the sugar until the mixture becomes thick and glossy. Add the flour and melted butter to the egg white mixture and mix until just combined. Allow the mixture to rest for about 15 minutes while you prepare your fortunes.

Preheat the oven to 350°F/180°C. Line a baking sheet with baking parchment.

Cut a piece of plain white paper into small strips about ¼in (5mm) wide and 1½in (4cm) long. Be imaginative and write some fortunes.

Spoon teaspoonfuls of the mixture on to the baking parchment and, using the back of a spoon, spread evenly and thinly to a circle about 3¼in (8cm) in diameter. Make sure the mixture is evenly spread to ease the next stage. You will need to work in batches: only bake three to four cookies per baking sheet. Bake for 3 minutes, or until lightly golden.

Remove from the oven and wait for 30 seconds before loosening the cookies using a flat palette knife. Return to the oven for a further 15–20 seconds to soften the cookies again. Remove from the oven and, working quickly, turn the cookies over and place a fortune in the center. Fold in half and half again. Set inside a small shot glass or bowl until cool and crisp. Repeat until all the mixture is used up.

Middle Eastern walnut and honey crisps

Spiced

This is based on a recipe of my grandmother's. Use the freshest walnuts you can find and the most flavorsome, fragrant honey.

Makes 18–24

1 stick (125g) **butter,** softened
½ cup (100g) **extra-fine sugar**
2 Tbsp **honey**
1¼ cups (150g) **all-purpose flour**
½ tsp **baking powder**
½ tsp **ground cinnamon**
½ tsp **ground ginger**
1 cup (100g) **freshly shelled walnuts,**
  roughly chopped

Preheat the oven to 350°F/180°C. Line one or two baking sheets with baking parchment.

Cream the butter and sugar in a large bowl until pale and creamy. Add the honey and beat for a further minute. In a separate bowl, combine the flour, baking powder, cinnamon and ginger. Stir into the butter mixture followed by the chopped walnuts. Mix until everything is just combined. Shape the mixture into tablespoon-sized balls and place on the prepared baking sheets. Press gently with a fork and bake for 12–15 minutes, or until golden.

Kourabiedes

Kourabiedes

Crumbly

These rich, short cookies are traditional Greek Christmas cookies and are perfect served with a nip of brandy.

Makes 20

1 stick (125g) **butter,** softened
½ cup (50g) **confectioners sugar,** plus extra for dusting
1 **egg yolk**
1 tsp **vanilla extract**
1 tsp **orange flower water**
1¼ cups (150g) **all-purpose flour**
1 tsp **baking powder**
generous 1 cup (150g) **ground almonds**

Preheat the oven to 325°F/160°C. Line two baking sheets with baking parchment.

Beat the butter until pale and creamy. Add the confectioners sugar, egg yolk, vanilla extract and orange flower water, and beat until fluffy. Combine the flour, baking powder and ground almonds in a separate bowl, then stir into the butter mixture. Using heaped tablespoonfuls of the dough, shape it into sausage shapes about 3¼in (8cm) long, then curve into a crescent shape on the baking sheet.

Bake for 15–18 minutes, or until light golden in color. Allow to cool for about 5 minutes on the baking sheet before dusting with extra confectioners sugar. Transfer to a wire rack and allow to cool completely.

Double ginger crackle cookies
Sweet ginger

This recipe comes from Grammy Brownlee, who makes these chewy cookies, studded with pieces of crystalized ginger, at Christmas-time. It's cookies like these that make you wish Christmas came more than once a year.

Makes 36

1½ sticks (160g) **butter**
1 cup (200g) **extra-fine sugar, plus**
  ½ cup (100g) **extra,** for rolling
1 **egg**
¼ cup (75ml) **molasses**
2¾ cup (300g) **all-purpose flour**
2 tsp **baking soda**
¼ tsp **salt**
1 Tbsp **ground ginger**
1 tsp **ground cinnamon**
1 tsp **ground cloves**
¾ cup (100g) **crystalized ginger,**
  finely chopped

Preheat the oven to 350°F/180°C.

In a large mixing bowl cream the butter and 7oz (200g) sugar until smooth. Beat in the egg and molasses until smooth. In a separate bowl, sift together the flour, baking soda, salt, ginger, cinnamon and cloves. Add to the butter mixture along with the crystalized ginger and stir just until combined.

Put the remaining sugar in a shallow bowl. Shape the dough into rounded tablespoon-sized balls (roughly 1½in/3.5cm wide) and roll the balls in sugar. Place the balls 2in (5cm) apart on ungreased or parchment-lined baking sheets.

Bake for 8–10 minutes, until the edges are cracked and the centers just set. Allow to cool on baking sheets for 5 minutes before transferring to wire racks to cool completely.

Portuguese star anise cookies

Licorice

I first stumbled upon these Portuguese cookies flavored with star anise while flipping through a Portuguese cookbook at the library. They are a traditional cookie, not necessarily festive in Portugal, but my version of the recipe has become part of our tea-time Christmas ritual. The addition of yeast, orange rind and a splash of port make for a very intriguing combination of flavors.

Makes 50–55

2 cups (400g) **plus** 1 tsp **extra-fine sugar**
½ cup (125ml) **lukewarm water**
1 Tbsp **fast-acting dried yeast**
5⅔ cup (650g) **all-purpose flour**
½ tsp **baking soda**
½ tsp **salt**
1 Tbsp **ground star anise**
1 tsp **ground cinnamon**
1 Tbsp **orange rind,** grated
2 **eggs**
1 tsp **vanilla extract**
2 Tbsp **vegetable oil**
1 Tbsp **port**
1 stick (120g) **butter,** melted and cooled

Preheat the oven to 350°F/180°C.

Dissolve 1 tsp sugar in lukewarm water. Sprinkle over the yeast and leave to stand for 10 minutes. Foam should appear over the surface.

Meanwhile, sift together the flour, baking soda, salt, ground star anise and cinnamon. Stir in the orange rind. Set aside.

In a separate bowl, whisk together the eggs, vanilla extract, vegetable oil, port and butter. Whisk the yeast mixture, and combine with the egg mixture. Gradually add to the flour mixture, stirring until the dough is combined.

Flour a work surface and knead the dough for 8–10 minutes. The dough will be quite stiff. Form into a ball and place in a lightly greased bowl. Cover with a tea towel and leave to rise for 1 hour. The dough will rise very little – don't panic!

Form the dough into rounded tablespoon-sized balls and place, 2in (5cm) apart, on greased or parchment-lined baking sheets.

Bake for 15 minutes, until golden. Allow to cool on the baking sheet then transfer to a wire rack and allow to cool completely.

Lavender sugar cookies

Dainty

Lavender buds lend a dainty quality to these traditional cookies. The flavor is created by blitzing in a food processor the buds with sugar and leaving them to infuse overnight. Lavender can, however, be omitted if a plain sugar cookie is required. Experiment with different shapes, sizes and decorations, depending on the celebration.

Makes approx. 48

1¼ cups (250g) **extra-fine sugar**
2 Tbsp **lavender buds**
2 sticks (220g) **butter, softened**
1 tsp **vanilla extract**
2¾ cups (300g) **all-purpose flour**
½ tsp **salt**
½ tsp **baking soda**

Place all the sugar and lavender buds in a food processor and blitz to break up the buds. Transfer the sugar to a covered container and allow to infuse, preferably overnight.

Pass the sugar through a sifter to remove the larger bud bits. Combine 1 cup (220g) sugar, butter and vanilla in a mixing bowl and, using an electric mixer, beat until smooth. In a separate bowl, sift together the flour, salt and baking soda. Using a wooden spoon, slowly stir the flour into the butter mixture until smooth. Divide the dough into two balls, cover with plastic wrap and chill for 1 hour.

Preheat the oven to 375°F/190°C. Lightly grease or line two baking trays with baking parchment.

Lightly flour a work surface and roll the balls, one at a time, to ⅛in (3mm) thick. Cut into shapes and sprinkle with the reserved sugar. Transfer to baking sheets. Bake for 8–12 minutes, until very lightly golden. The exact timing will depend on the size of the shapes.

Allow to cool on the baking sheets for a few minutes, then transfer to wire racks and allow to cool completely.

Lavender sugar cookies

Orange and rum shortbread

Decadent

This recipe is a variation on our Classic shortbread featured in the Coffee-time chapter (see page 115). Light, buttery shortbread coupled with a splash of rum and candied orange peel is as festive as it gets. The crown of creamy icing is just the icing on the, well, shortbread.

Makes 40 x 2-in (5-cm) diameter cookies

scant ½ cup (50g) **confectioners sugar**, sifted
2 cups (450g) **butter, softened**
1½ Tbsp **dark rum**
4⅔ cups (525g) **all-purpose flour,** sifted
½ cup (60g) **cornstarch**, sifted
1 cup (200g) **store-bought candied orange peel**, finely chopped

Preheat the oven to 350°F/180°C. Line two baking sheets with baking parchment.

Combine the confectioners sugar and butter in a large mixing bowl and beat until very light and fluffy. Beat in the rum. In a separate bowl combine the flour and cornstarch. Using a wooden spoon, stir the flour mixture into the butter mixture and work together until combined. Stir in the candied orange peel.

Gather the dough and divide into two equal mounds. Flour a work surface and roll the first mound into a 9½-in (24-cm) wide circle, almost ⅝in (1.5cm) thick. Cut the dough into the desired shapes and place on parchment-lined baking sheets. (We used a 2-in [5-cm] wide round cookie cutter.)

Bake for 20–22 minutes, until slightly golden. Allow to cool for 5 minutes, then transfer to wire racks and allow to cool completely. Meanwhile, continue baking the remaining shortbread.

Top, if desired, with Vanilla butter icing (see page 166) and our Candied peel (see page 168).

Fruitcake cookies

Moist

I must admit that fruitcake was never my idea of festive bliss. Until, that is, I tasted it in cookie form!

Makes 40

½ cup (50g) **whole hazelnuts**
1 stick (110g) **butter**
½ cup (70g) **dark brown sugar**
1 **egg**
1¼ cups (145g) **all-purpose flour**
½ tsp **baking soda**
⅛ tsp **salt**
generous ½ cup (375g) **dates**, finely chopped
1 cup (175g) **candied peel**
½ cup (50g) **walnut pieces**
½ cup (50g) **pecan nuts**, chopped

Preheat the oven to 350°F/180°C.

Toast the whole hazelnuts in a dry frying pan on the stove until fragrant and slightly golden. Tip into a clean tea towel and rub the nuts together to loosen and remove the skins. Skins are stubborn, so don't worry if bits remain.

Cream the butter and brown sugar in an electric mixer until light and fluffy. Add the egg and beat until smooth. Sift the flour with the baking soda and salt. Stir into the butter mixture just until combined. In a separate bowl, mix the dates, candied peel and nuts. Stir into the batter. The dough will be heavy on fruit and nuts, light on batter.

Roll the dough into teaspoon-sized balls and place on lightly greased or parchment-lined baking sheets. Bake for 12 minutes until golden, but slightly soft in the center. Allow to cool on the baking sheets for 5 minutes, then transfer to wire racks and allow to cool completely.

Store in an airtight container for up to 5 days, or freeze for up to 2 months.

Coconut date balls

Rich

These wonderfully sweet, coconut-covered balls are an essential addition to any festive sweet tray. The recipe has been handed down through the family from my great-grandmother Brownlee. I wonder if she used Rice Krispies® way back then?

Makes approx. 24

1½ cups (220g) **extra-fine sugar**
2 **eggs,** lightly beaten
1 cup (150g) **dates,** finely chopped
1 tsp **vanilla extract**
½ cup (80g) **Rice Krispies®**
½ cup (50g) **walnuts,** chopped
1½ cups (100g) **sweetened shredded coconut**

Line two baking sheets with wax paper or baking parchment.

Combine the sugar, beaten eggs and chopped dates in a large saucepan. Place the pan over medium heat and cook the mixture, stirring occasionally, for 7 minutes. Remove from the heat and add the vanilla extract, Rice Krispies® and walnuts. Stir well. Allow to cool for 10–15 minutes.

Place the coconut in a shallow bowl. Wet your hands with cold water and roll the date mixture into small, teaspoon-sized balls. The mixture will be sticky, so keep cold water on hand. Roll the balls in coconut and place on the baking sheets. Allow balls to firm up at room temperature.

Store in airtight containers for up to 5 days, the layers separated by wax paper, or freeze for up to 2 months.

Chocolate peanut butter balls

Dangerous

Christmas wouldn't be Christmas without feasting on these decadent balls on Christmas Eve at my grandmother's house. They were also the most popular dessert at my wedding. The recipe can be doubled, tripled or even quadrupled, and freezes well.

Makes approx. 40 rounded tablespoon-sized balls or 60–70 rounded teaspoon-sized balls

generous 1 cup (250g) **creamy peanut butter**
4 Tbsp **butter**, softened
1 cup (125g) **confectioners sugar**
½ cup (50g) **walnuts**, chopped and toasted
¾ cup (50g) **sweetened shredded coconut**
2 Tbsp **Rice Krispies®**

For the coating:
generous 1 cup (200g) **chocolate chips or unsweetened baking chocolate**, roughly chopped
1 Tbsp **butter**

Line two baking sheets with wax paper or baking parchment.

Combine the peanut butter, butter and confectioners sugar in a large mixing bowl and stir well until smooth. Add the walnuts, coconut and Rice Krispies®, and stir until combined. Cover and chill for 1 hour.

To make the coating, combine the chocolate and butter in a heatproof bowl over a saucepan of simmering water. Stir until melted and remove from the heat.

Form the peanut butter mixture into tablespoon-sized balls and, using two spoons, dip the balls into chocolate. Place on the baking sheets. If the chocolate gets thick, place the bowl over simmering water and re-heat. Chill the balls for 30 minutes then store.

Store the balls layered between wax paper in airtight containers in the fridge for up to 1 week. Alternatively, freeze for up to 2 months.

Valentine stained glass cookies

Valentine stained glass cookies

Eye-catching

These little gems are almost too pretty to eat!

Makes approx. 40

1 stick (110g) **butter, softened**
generous ½ cup (110g) **extra-fine
  sugar**
½ cup (125ml) **honey**
1 **egg**
1 tsp **vanilla extract**
4 cups (450g) **all-purpose flour**
1 tsp **baking powder**
½ tsp **baking soda**
½ tsp **salt**
Approx. 40 pieces **hard candy**

Cream the butter, sugar, honey, egg
and vanilla extract until smooth. In
a separate bowl, sift the flour,
baking powder, baking soda and salt.
Add to the butter mixture and stir to
combine. Gather the dough into a ball
in the bowl and chill for 2 hours.

Preheat the oven to 350°F/180°C.
Line two baking sheets with foil,
shiny-side up.

Lightly flour a work surface and roll out
the dough ½in (1cm) thick. Using lightly
floured 2½ –3¼-in (6–8-cm) heart-
shaped cutters, cut out heart shapes.
Cut a smaller heart shape within the
cookie, leaving a ⅝–¾-in (1.5–2-cm)
border of dough. (This is easily done
by making a cardboard heart-shaped
cut-out and tracing around it with a
knife.) Remove the center of each
heart and set aside. Place the cut-outs
on the baking sheets.

Crush the sweets between two sheets
of wax paper or baking parchment
using a rolling pin or mallet. Spoon into
the center of the hearts. Bake for 6–8
minutes, until the sweets have melted
and the cookies are golden. Allow the
cookies to cool completely before
removing them carefully from the foil
using a spatula.

Meanwhile, gather up any dough
scraps and re-roll to make more
cookies. Only re-roll the dough once;
any more and it will become too tough.

Easter lemon curd sandwiches
Delicate

Easter-time treats, for me, aren't just about chocolate. They can also mean fresh flavors and pretty delicacies that signify spring. Here it is, in cookie form!

Makes 18–24

1 **quantity** *Langues de chat*,
   baked and cooled **(see page 123)**

For the lemon curd:
1 stick (100g) **unsalted butter**
¾ cup (150g) **extra-fine sugar**
Juice and grated rind of 3 **lemons**
3 **eggs,** beaten

Make the lemon curd: put the butter, sugar, lemon juice and rind in a heatproof bowl. Place over a saucepan of simmering water and stir over low heat until the sugar has dissolved and the mixture is warm. Whisk the warm lemon mixture into the beaten eggs and strain through a non-metallic sieve. Return the mixture to the heatproof bowl and place over the still simmering water. Stir occasionally until the mixture thickens and coats the back of a wooden spoon. Do not allow the mixture to boil or it will curdle.

Spoon the lemon curd into a bowl and allow to cool. If making the curd in advance, pour the mixture into hot, sterilized jars and seal well. The lemon curd will keep for up to 1 month, stored in a cool place.

Line two baking sheets with wax paper. Place half of the *langues de chat* underside-up on the paper. Spoon the lemon curd into a piping bag fitted with a plain tip (or a plastic bag with the corner snipped off). Pipe the lemon curd onto the *langues de chat*, then top with other *langues de chat*, rounded-side up, to form a sandwich.

The sandwiched cookies will keep, layered between sheets of wax paper or baking parchment in an airtight container in the fridge, for 24 hours. Before serving, dust the sandwiches liberally with confectioners sugar.

Easter lemon curd sandwiches

Rugelach

Rugelach

Warming

Rugelach is a traditional Jewish holiday cookie with jam, nuts, raisins and cinnamon within a soft dough. They are worth the effort, any time of the year.

Makes 48

For the dough:
1 cup (225-g tub) **cream cheese**
2 sticks (220g) **unsalted butter**
¼ cup (50g) **extra-fine sugar**
1 tsp **vanilla extract**
3 cups (325g) **all-purpose flour**
¼ tsp **salt**

For the filling:
½ cup (75g) **extra-fine sugar**
½ cup (50g) **light brown sugar**
½ tsp **ground cinnamon**
scant ½ cup (100g) **raisins**
¾ cup (100g) **walnuts, chopped**
½ cup (110g) **apricot jam**

For the topping:
¼ cup (75 ml) **milk**
2 Tbsp **extra-fine sugar**
1 tsp **ground cinnamon**

Line a baking sheet with baking parchment. In a mixing bowl blend the cream cheese and butter until soft. Beat in the sugar and vanilla extract. Slowly add the flour and salt until incorporated. Divide the dough into four portions and cover each with plastic wrap. Refrigerate for at least 2 hours.

To make the filling combine the sugars, cinnamon, raisins and walnuts in a bowl and stir until well combined.

Remove the dough from the fridge and allow to stand for 15 minutes until it is soft enough to roll. Preheat the oven to 350°F/180°C.

Lightly flour a work surface and roll out each dough portion into a 8½-in (22-cm) circle. Spread the dough evenly with 2 Tbsp of the apricot jam. Sprinkle a quarter of the raisin-walnut filling over the jam and press it down firmly and evenly. Using a sharp knife, cut each dough circle into 12 pieces as if you were cutting a cake. Starting at the wide end, roll up each triangle and bend the ends around to form a slight crescent shape.

Place the Rugelach, point underneath, about 1½in (6cm) apart, on the baking sheet. Refrigerate for at least 30 minutes, or until firm.

Brush the Rugelach with milk, then sprinkle over the sugar and cinnamon. Bake for 18–20 minutes, or until lightly browned. Using a small spatula, transfer the cookies to wire racks and allow to cool completely. Dust with confectioners sugar to serve.

Icings and extras

Colored icings

Yield 6oz (175g)

generous 1 cup (150g) **confectioners sugar**
2–3 Tbsp **water**
3–4 **drops food coloring of your choice**

Sift the confectioners sugar into a mixing bowl and stir in the water until the consistency is smooth and shiny but not too runny. Add the your chosen color and mix until the color is even.

■ *For a more sophisticated icing, add 2–3 Tbsp liqueur instead of the water.*

Royal eggnog icing

Yield – enough to decorate Gingerbread men generously (see page 90)

generous 2 cups (300g) **confectioners sugar**
2 Tbsp **meringue powder (optional)**
¼ cup (75ml) **eggnog**

Sift the confectioners sugar with the meringue powder into a mixing bowl and stir in the eggnog until the consistency is smooth and shiny but not too runny. Correct the consistency by adding more confectioners sugar or eggnog.

■ *Meringue powder stabilizes icing and makes it behave. Look for it where cake decorating equipment is sold.*

Lemon icing

Yield 6oz (175g)

generous 1 cup (150g) **confectioners sugar**
2–3 Tbsp **lemon juice**
Grated rind of 1 **lemon (optional)**

Sift the confectioners sugar into a mixing bowl and stir in the lemon juice until the consistency is smooth and shiny but not too runny. Spoon the mixture onto the cookies and spread evenly. Top with additional toppings if desired and leave to set.

■ *This can be made using oranges or limes as an alternative*

Chocolate icing

Yield 6oz (175g)

generous 1 cup (150g) **confectioners sugar**
1½–2 Tbsp **cocoa powder**
1 tsp **butter, softened**
3–4 Tbsp **water**

Sift the confectioners sugar and cocoa powder into a mixing bowl. Add the softened butter and water, stirring until the consistency is smooth and shiny. Spoon the mixture onto the cookies and spread evenly.

Vanilla butter icing

Yield approx. 8oz (225g)

¼ stick (40g) **unsalted butter,** softened
1½ cups (175g) **confectioners sugar,** sifted
1–2 drops **vanilla extract**
1–1½ Tbsp **light cream or milk**

Mix the butter vigorously until very soft and creamy. Gradually stir in the sifted confectioners sugar and vanilla extract. Mix to a smooth paste, adding the cream or milk as needed.

■ *You can color or flavor this icing as liked by adding a few drops of food coloring or grated citrus rind.*

Chocolate ganache

Ganache is a French term referring to a smooth mixture of chopped chocolate and heavy cream. Butter can be added to give the ganache a shiny glaze that won't dull. Always choose a chocolate that you like the taste of because this is what will determine the taste and quality of your ganache.

A general guideline:
To make a glaze or coating: 1 part cream to 3 parts chocolate.
To make a rich truffle filling: 1 part cream to 2 parts chocolate.
To make a light filling: 1 part cream to 1 part chocolate.

Yield 6oz (175g)

3½oz (100g) **plain, milk or white chocolate,** chopped
¼ cup (60ml) **heavy cream**
1 Tbsp (15g) **butter**

Place the chocolate in a medium-sized bowl. Set aside. Heat the cream and butter in a small saucepan over medium heat. Bring just to a boil. Immediately pour the boiling cream over the chocolate and allow to stand for 5 minutes. Stir with a whisk until smooth. A teaspoon of liqueur or flavoring can be added at this stage if liked.

Colored sugars

Yield 1¾oz (50g)

scant ½ cup (50g) **extra-fine sugar**
3–4 drops **food coloring**

Place extra-fine sugar into a jar with a secure lid. Add food coloring of your choice. Tighten the lid and shake vigorously for a couple of minutes or until the sugar is evenly colored.

Use colored sugars to sprinkle over still warm cookies or sprinkle over freshly iced or glazed cookies and leave to set.

Flavored sugars

Vanilla – put a vanilla pod into a jar of extra-fine sugar and leave to infuse for at least 1 week, shaking occasionally.

Lavender – add about 4–5 heads of fresh, unsprayed lavender to a jar of extra-fine sugar and leave to infuse for 3 days.

Spiced – combine about ½ tsp pumpkin-pie spice or cinnamon to scant ½ cup (50g) extra-fine sugar and mix to combine. Alternatively, place whole cinnamon sticks or cloves into a jar of extra-fine sugar and leave to infuse for 1–2 weeks.

Citrus – add 1–2 large pieces of citrus rind to a jar of extra-fine sugar and leave to infuse for 3–4 days, shaking occasionally.

Dipping chocolate

Dipping cookies in chocolate can be a quick and easy way to add the "wow" factor. Place dipped cookies on a sheet of baking parchment and leave until set.

To melt chocolate in the microwave: place the chocolate in a microwave-safe bowl. Microwave on medium power for 1 minute then stir. Repeat the process, stirring after every 30 seconds until the chocolate has melted.

To melt chocolate on top of the stove: place the chocolate in a heatproof bowl that fits snugly on top of a saucepan. Bring a small quantity of water to a simmer in the saucepan and place the bowl on top. Reduce the heat and stir the chocolate until smooth and melted. Carefully remove from the heat and set aside.

To melt chocolate in the oven: place the chocolate in a heatproof bowl in an oven preheated to the lowest temperature. Stir occasionally until the chocolate has melted. This usually takes about 5–10 minutes.

Candied peel

Yield 7oz (200g)

4–6 **citrus fruits** (a mixture of grapefruit, oranges, lemons, limes), unwaxed and
    preferably organic (if not, wash fruit very well)
1 cup (200g) **sugar**
scant 1 cup (200ml) **water**
½ cup (100g) **extra-fine sugar,** for coating

Using a wide, horizontal vegetable peeler, peel the skin from the fruit, making sure not to peel away the bitter white pith. Finely slice the peel into matchsticks, or julienne strips. Set aside. Combine the sugar and water in a heavy-bottomed saucepan and bring to a boil. Boil the mixture gently until the sugar dissolves. Add the chopped peel, reduce the heat and simmer gently for 45 minutes. Remove the peel with a slotted spoon and place on a paper towel to cool. Place the remaining sugar in a bowl. Toss the cooled peel in the sugar, then leave to dry on a clean tea towel.

Store in an airtight container. Candied peel will keep for several months.

Clear sugar glaze

A sugar glaze can give a cookie a shiny, glossy finish. Combine 1 part sugar to 2 parts water in a small saucepan. Bring to a boil, then simmer over moderate heat for about 5 minutes or until reduced by half. Remove from the heat and allow to cool. To 3 Tbsp syrup add about ¾ cup (100g) sifted confectioners sugar and mix until dissolved. Brush the glaze over still warm cookies and leave to set.

Stencil patterns

Stencil patterns can be bought from most kitchen stores or, alternatively, can be made easily at home. Use thin cardboard or baking parchment and cut out shapes or patterns. Hold the stencils over the cookies and gently sift icing sugar or cocoa powder through a fine sifter to fill the uncovered surface. Gently remove the stencil and be careful not to stack the cookies. Make sure there is a contrast between the color of the cookie and the dusting ingredient.

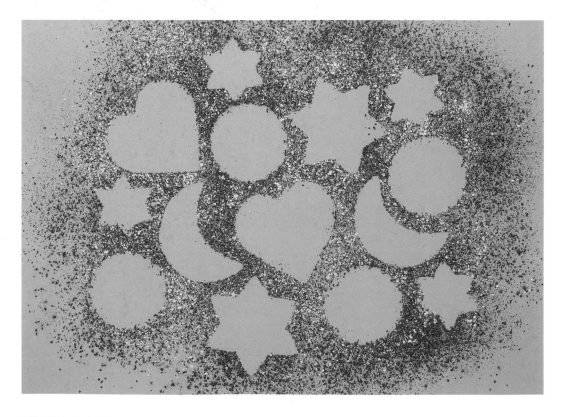

About the authors

New Zealand-born Pippa Cuthbert's passion for food and cooking began at a very young age. With degrees in both human nutrition and food science, Pippa has gone on to build a successful career as a food stylist, food writer and home economist, working on books, magazines, TV commercials, packaging and advertorials. Complemented by each other's backgrounds, interests and skills, Pippa and Lindsay have now produced *Cookies!*

Food and writing are Lindsay Cameron Wilson's passions. She blended the two in college where she studied history, journalism and the culinary arts. In 2001, Lindsay left her job as a food columnist in Halifax, Nova Scotia, and moved to London. That's when she met Pippa, and the work for their first book, *Juice!,* began. The two have since moved on to *Ice Cream!*, *Soup!*, *Grill!*, *Pizza!* and now *Cookies!* Lindsay continues to work as a food journalist in Canada, where she lives with her husband James, and sons Luke and Charlie.

Index